Vegetation Classification Guidelines

National Park Service Vegetation Inventory, Version 2.0

Natural Resource Report NPS/NRPC/NRR—2011/374

Chris Lea

National Park Service
Vegetation Inventory
P.O. Box 25287 (Academy Place)
Denver, CO 80225

April 2011

U.S. Department of the Interior
National Park Service
Natural Resource Program Center
Fort Collins, Colorado

The National Park Service, Natural Resource Program Center publishes a range of reports that address natural resource topics of interest and applicability to a broad audience in the National Park Service and others in natural resource management, including scientists, conservation and environmental constituencies, and the public.

Natural Resource Reports are the designated medium for disseminating high priority, current natural resource information with managerial application. The targets a general, diverse audience, and may contain NPS policy considerations or address sensitive issues of management applicability.

All manuscripts in the series receive the appropriate level of peer review to ensure that the information is scientifically credible, technically accurate, appropriately written for the intended audience, and designed and published in a professional manner.

This report received formal peer review by subject-matter experts who were not directly involved in the collection, analysis, or reporting of the data, and whose background and expertise put them on par technically and scientifically with the authors of the information.

Views, statements, findings, conclusions, recommendations, and data in this report do not necessarily reflect views and policies of the National Park Service, U.S. Department of the Interior. Mention of trade names or commercial products does not constitute endorsement or recommendation for use by the U.S. Government.

This report is available from the National Park Service Vegetation Inventory website (http://science.nature.nps.gov/im/inventory/veg/index.cfm) and from the Natural Resource Publications Management website (http://www.nature.nps.gov/publications/nrpm/).

Please cite this publication as:

Lea, C. 2011. Vegetation classification guidelines: National Park Service Vegetation Inventory, version 2.0. Natural Resource Report NPS/NRPC/NRR—2011/374. National Park Service, Fort Collins, Colorado.

NPS 909/107410, April 2011

Contents

Contents (continued)

Contents (continued)

Contents (continued)

Figures

vii

Tables

Executive Summary

The objective of the National Park Service (NPS) Vegetation Inventory is to classify vegetation as ecological community types in each of more than 250 NPS Inventory and Monitoring park units ("parks") in the United States outside of Alaska and to map vegetation to that classification scheme developed for the unit. This guidance is a revision and update of the 1994 guidance on vegetation classification within the NPS Vegetation Inventory (The Nature Conservancy and Environmental Systems Research Institute 1994) and supersedes the 1994 version.

This guidance should be read and referred to by all NPS staff and cooperators who apply vegetation classification within NPS Vegetation Inventory projects or who oversee such projects. In addition, this guidance may prove useful for other individuals or organizations who may need to apply the science of vegetation classification to resource inventory, mapping, and/or management activities. It is directed at professional vegetation ecologists and assumes that the reader has a basic understanding of vegetation ecology, including vegetation classification, and is more for developers of, rather than users of, vegetation classification products.

Chapter 1 provides the context of vegetation classification, both within the NPS and in the agency's role in development of national standards for vegetation classification. It describes important changes in approach from that of the 1994 version, and outlines requirements for projects funded by the NPS Vegetation Inventory.

Chapter 2 provides information for "best practices" approaches to vegetation classification that NPS has found to be useful to site-based resource inventory and management. It reviews and briefly describes common vegetation classification methods, but is not a treatise on them. A number of manuals and papers on classification methods are referenced.

Chapter 3 describes how vegetation classes derived from the methods described in Chapter 2 may be applied to map classes, especially for common problems in achieving a 1:1 relationship between the two.

Chapter 4 describes reporting requirements for vegetation classification products developed by the NPS Vegetation Inventory.

Chapter 5 describes considerations and methods for developing diagnostic field keys to vegetation classes. While not part of a vegetation classification *per se*, field keys are important tools in successfully applying a vegetation classification scheme that has been derived from field-observed data to vegetation mapping, including the assessment of a vegetation map.

Appendix A describes the history of the National Vegetation Classification Standard (NVCS) and its prescribed taxonomic content, the United States National Vegetation Classification (USNVC) and the relationship of the NPS Vegetation Inventory to them.

Appendix B is a glossary of vegetation classification terms.

Appendix C and Appendix D provide examples of vegetation descriptions and diagnostic field keys, respectively.

Acknowledgments

David Tart (U.S. Forest Service), Jim Drake (NatureServe), John Dennis (National Park Service), and Karl Brown (National Park Service) reviewed early drafts of this report and provided comments that greatly improved its quality. Steve Fancy (National Park Service) served as peer review manager for the report.

Members of the Ecological Society of America Panel on Vegetation Classification (http://www.esa.org/vegweb/) and of the Vegetation Subcommittee of the Federal Geographic Data Committee (http://www.fgdc.gov/participation/working-groups-subcommittees/vsc/index_html), and many cooperators of the NPS Vegetation Inventory provided useful discussions and ideas that have been incorporated into this guidance

The authors of the first version of this guidance, Dennis Grossman, Kathleen Lemon Goodin, Xiaojun Li, Don Faber-Langendoen, and Mark Anderson are recognized for developing a foundation for vegetation classification from which this guidance continues.

Funding for the development and testing of many of the methods in this document and for the writing of the guidance itself was provided by the National Park Service Inventory and Monitoring Program.

1.0 Introduction

1.1 Purposes of Vegetation Classification

This report guides the ecological classification of vegetation for purposes of the National Park Service (NPS) Vegetation Inventory.

In a resource management and inventory context, the ecological classification of vegetation seeks to simplify the complex multiple-species continuum that represents the concept of vegetation into generalized and discrete taxonomic classes that are recognizable by different observers. Vegetation classes allow observers and managers to use a manageable number of names and concepts in describing and communicating about vegetation and to communicate complex ecological concepts more consistently. In accomplishing this purpose, classification must make generalizations about plant communities and must impose somewhat arbitrary boundaries between classes in order to distinguish between them.

Vegetation classification in the NPS Vegetation Inventory serves three major purposes, which follow.

Description: Describing taxonomic classes of vegetation provides a framework of units with narrow enough limits from which vegetation in a park can be described, based on its floristic, structural, environmental, and geographic range attributes. Description may be qualitative (e.g., written syntheses of observations) or quantitative (e.g., synthesis tables from plot data) or a combination of both.

Diagnosis: Defining limits to discrete taxonomic classes enables users to differentiate between one set of ecological conditions and another. A field key to vegetation types represents a formal diagnosis of vegetation.

Inventory: The combination of description and diagnosis allows vegetation to be recognized repeatably within and among parks and, thus, for vegetation to be inventoried. Such an inventory may be conducted in the field or from remotely sensed data (vegetation mapping). The NPS Vegetation Inventory has a spatial component (i.e., a map of vegetation classes), as well as an attribute component (descriptions and diagnoses of those classes).

1.2 Legal and Policy Basis for Vegetation Classification in the National Park Service

The National Parks Omnibus Management Act of 1998 (16 USC § 5904) established specific legal authority and responsibility for the NPS, through the Secretary of the Interior, to implement an inventorying and monitoring program for natural resources within National Park system units. These variously designated units, which include National Monuments, National Historic Sites, National Historical Parks, National Recreation Area, National Seashores, National Preserves, Parkways, and others, are generalized to the term of "parks" for purposes of this document. The NPS had previously established a vegetation mapping program as one of several basic inventory themes for parks with significant natural resources (National Park Service 1992).

While the primary purpose of the National Park Service Vegetation Inventory is to provide spatial and attribute information about vegetation within parks, executive directives require coordination of this purpose with other federal activities. Office of Management and Budget Circular 16, originally issued in 1953, and revised in 1967, 1990, and 2002 (Office of Management and Budget 1990, 2002) directs federal agencies to coordinate spatial data development. The 1990 revision established the Federal Geographic Data Committee, an office within the U.S. Geological Survey that is charged with oversight of development of federal geospatial standards and with the facilitation of federal and non-federal coordination and cooperation in standards development.

Specifically, Circular 16 directs federal agencies to "…collect, maintain, disseminate, and preserve spatial information such that the resulting data, information, or products can be readily shared with other federal agencies and non-federal users, and promote data integration between all sources…" and to "…coordinate and work in partnership with federal, state, tribal and local government agencies, academia and the private sector to efficiently and cost-effectively collect, integrate, maintain, disseminate, and preserve spatial data, building upon local data wherever possible" (Office of Management and Budget 2002).

Pursuant to Circular 16, the National Park Service coordinates its internal vegetation classification and mapping activities and contributes to the development of the United States National Vegetation Classification (USNVC) (Federal Geographic Data Committee 1997, 2008, Jennings et al. 2009) through its membership and representation on the Vegetation Subcommittee of the Federal Geographic Data Committee. Additionally, the NPS currently is active in national standards development through the Vegetation Panel of the Ecological Society of America (Peet 2008).

Appendix A describes the history of the National Vegetation Classification Standard (NVCS) and the current relationship of the NPS Vegetation Inventory to the development of the USNVC, which is the vegetation classification (taxonomic) content that is prescribed by the NVCS (Federal Geographic Data Committee 2008).

The user of this guidance should be aware that, following the revision of the NVCS in 2008, many rapid changes in the content of the USNVC and in the serving of that content have occurred and are still occurring. Parts of this guidance may become obsolete within a number of years after its publication. NPS project investigators and managers should consult the NPS Vegetation Inventory web site (http://science.nature.nps.gov/im/veg/index.cfm) periodically.

1.3 The Importance of a Field-based Vegetation Classification

An essential part of the products of the NPS Vegetation Inventory is an ecological classification of the vegetation of each park. A rigorous classification scheme that is based on quantitative data gives informative attribute context to the classes of the vegetation map of the park. Additionally, while a vegetation map is a representation of vegetation distribution at a single point in time that may become progressively outdated with ecological succession and disturbance, the ecological classification itself is relatively "timeless," as updated maps can be based on the original classification. Thus, the ecological classification is the true "inventory" product of the NPS Vegetation Inventory.

The NPS Vegetation Inventory maps vegetation in parks using an *a priori vegetation* classification scheme that is developed from comprehensive floristic data (i.e., species composition, including the presence and abundance of individual plant species, and vegetation physiognomy and structure). The data are collected by observers in the field at those parks. Map classes are either equivalent to the field-derived vegetation classes or are mutually exclusive and explicit combinations of these vegetation classes. In contrast, many vegetation mapping efforts classify vegetation with a primary emphasis on remotely sensed attributes of vegetation or from a more qualitative field perspective.

The *a priori* classification approach from field data has several benefits. First, map classes based on data that are based on a field-based view of vegetation will be more interpretable to the experience of a field-based user of the maps. Second, the map classes will be less subject to effects of mapping methodology, including variation in imagery used for mapping; different mapping projects that are based on the same *a priori* classification will provide more methodological consistency and more comparable maps (Tart et al. 2005). This is an important benefit, whether the projects are at different sites or at the same site at different times. Third, while individual vegetation stands may change in extent or position over relatively short times due to stochastic or gradual environmental changes, rendering a map obsolete, a classification is more robust to change. This is analogous to the long-term consistency in a taxonomic species concept despite short-term changes within individual populations of that species due to births, deaths, and movements of individuals and founding and extirpation events. Fourth, the classification is important in itself as a documentation of the vegetation composition of a site at a point in time, with plot data serving as (and analogous to) voucher specimens often collected for biological inventories. Finally, the archived field plot data can be re-analyzed, re-synthesized, and re-interpreted in the future and/or on a larger geographic scale than the inventory site (the park) and can contribute to ongoing vegetation classification work in the public interest.

1.4 Changes from Previous Version of this Report

The 1994 version of this guidance (The Nature Conservancy and Environmental Systems Research Institute 1994) focused primarily on the early development of the then nascent National Vegetation Classification Standard (NVCS) along with its taxonomic content, the United States National Vegetation Classification (USNVC). In consideration of greater partner involvement in the development of the USNVC since 1994 (Federal Geographic Data Committee 1997, 2008, Grossman et al. 1998, Peet 2008, Faber-Langendoen et al. 2009, Jennings et al. 2009, NatureServe 2009), and of experience by the NPS in applying a "top-down" approach to classification intended to guide local mapping, NPS has revised this guidance to focus more on internal agency needs and to apply its experience more on site-specific resource inventories than on support of the USNVC. The focus of this version of classification guidance is on applying a vegetation classification for resource management and inventory, including vegetation mapping. In addition, it prescribes requirements of projects funded by the NPS Vegetation Inventory. In those respects, this version is an agency procedures and best practices document, similar in scope and intent to that of Tart et al. (2005).

Nevertheless, the NPS continues to support USNVC development and has, in fact, increased its support of that function in recent years, through its active participation on the FGDC Vegetation Subcommittee and the Ecological Society of America Vegetation Panel and its funding support of partnership initiatives to develop the new [2008] USNVC hierarchy, particularly at levels that correspond to more easily mapped vegetation units. The current guidance also continues to advocate use of the USNVC content, whenever feasible, to meet NPS inventory objectives.

The Nature Conservancy and Environmental Systems Research Institute (1994) prescribed a "top-down" approach of vegetation classification and mapping, whereby nationally recognized USNVC content would form the *a priori* basis for vegetation and map classes and that units at specific levels of the hierarchy (e.g., the USNVC association or alliance) would be the basis for map classes. Experience with this approach revealed several difficulties related to the early stage of development of the USNVC. First, the relatively experimental nature of relating the lower (floristic) levels of USNVC alliance and USNVC association to map classes probably created overly optimistic expectations of performance of these hierarchy units as map classes. Attempting to map at these levels, particularly in the western states, often caused a proliferation of map classes that, individually, could not be mapped accurately from remotely sensed data. Second, use of the [original] upper [physiognomic] levels of the USNVC as a solution to the difficulties encountered with the floristic levels proved to be inadequate as an alternative solution because the classified units of these physiognomic levels often did not relate to ecologically meaningful gradients (Faber-Langendoen et al. 2008, Federal Geographic Data Committee 2008). Third, the finding of apparent regional discrepancies in ecological and mapping scaling of floristic units of the USNVC (alliance and association) as they were being applied between eastern and western sites (Lea 2008, 2009) probably created confusion as to what floristic levels might serve as reasonably few and reasonably accurate map classes. Finally, the nascent status of the USNVC meant that type concepts were often based on qualitative assessments or on more quantitative, but geographically limited and biased data. These conditions meant that national descriptions were often too broad or too inaccurate to apply to the specific conditions needed for individual park projects, especially for the recognition of diagnostic conditions.

For purposes of completing the NPS Vegetation Inventory, this guidance emphasizes a "bottom-up," rather than "top-down," approach to vegetation classification. Classified vegetation units for parks should be developed from local vegetation data, and then cross walked to current content of the USNVC (NatureServe 2009, Faber-Langendoen et al. 2010) at the appropriate hierarchy level. Park projects should strive for a consistent level of classification within the current USNVC hierarchy; this level may vary with geographical region of the United States. Most vegetation classes within that level should be *generally* feasible to map (e.g., at least a 60% thematic accuracy). While mapping feasibility should guide the hierarchy level selected for classification, it should not influence the decision to recognize individual ecological classes of vegetation within that hierarchy level for the ecological classification. Thus, most, but not necessarily all, vegetation classes that are described for a park should be feasible to map individually. Many riparian and wetland vegetation community types, in particular, occur in recognizable patches that are smaller than most practical minimum mapping unit sizes for a remotely sensed mapping approach, while their upland counterparts often occur in patches large enough to map.

For guidance for investigators who are familiar with the USNVC content, it has proven to be generally feasible to map at the current content (NatureServe 2009) of the USNVC level of association in the eastern United States and in the Great Plains, since, at the scale of most parks, most alliances have only a single association represented. This scenario is as was expected by The Nature Conservancy and Environmental Systems Research Institute et al. (1994). In the western states (the Rocky Mountains and trans-Pecos Texas to the Pacific coast), alliances are often represented by many associations, and mapped vegetation classes have generally been cross walked to the level of the USNVC alliance or coarser (NPS data). Thus, described vegetation classes (and most map classes) will often be equivalent to USNVC associations in eastern or Great Plains parks, but may be at the USNVC alliance or the USNVC group level for western areas. This approach does not preclude recognition of finer vegetation classes (e.g., cross walking of some individual plots); it does prescribe that allocation of vegetation plots per vegetation class and the classification and description of vegetation will focus on the expected consistent hierarchy level of thematic map resolution.

1.5 Key Requirements of the Park-based Classification

- The classification system must be floristically based (classification units are grouped and differentiated by the plant species composition of the classified units). Obvious physiognomic and structural criteria (e.g., tree-dominated versus shrub- or herb-dominated versus lichen-dominated) are also used, where applicable.

- Vegetation classification (taxonomic) units and descriptions will be representative of vegetation as it can be observed within the park (this representation may be of broader geographical extent than the park, but must include the area of the park).

- The classification units must be ecologically meaningful and represent plant communities that occur across the landscape of the park.

- The classification must be derived from quantitative field sampling and must describe vegetation so that it can be identified readily at the geographic scale of the park. The full set of data that are used for the classification may be constrained to areas within the park or they may be supplemented by plots that were previously collected at a geographically larger scale than the park. Collection of new field data funded by the NPS Vegetation Inventory will generally be limited to the park, but a minority of new data may be collected from the immediate park environs, if an adequate number of stands needed to provide an adequate description of vegetation classes that occur within the park cannot be found within the park. (In contrast, mapping is limited strictly to authorized park boundaries, unless partners can contribute to costs of environs mapping). Unless otherwise not feasible, each vegetation class will be represented by at least one plot from the park.

- The thematic level (e.g., in the USNVC hierarchy) for sampling and describing individual vegetation types must be appropriate scaled, so that *most* of vegetation types at that level that are them are effectively mappable as individual types from stands that are discernable on remote sensing imagery, can effectively be modeled as map classes from remotely sensed data, or both, with an expected overall thematic accuracy (Czaplewski 2003, Lea and Curtis 2010) of at least 60%. It is not required that *all* types that are identified at the primary classified and described level be individually mappable. It is recognized that ecologically valid, but difficult-to-map units occur at nearly all levels of any ecologically-based classification, including the USNVC.

- Classified vegetation types at a thematic level that is finer than that which can be mapped effectively may be recognized as occurring in the park, but should not form the basis for the park descriptions. For example, if it is determined that USNVC group units are the thematically finest level that will largely provide [mostly] mappable units, then the park descriptions should be at the group level. Individual USNVC associations that are members of these groups and are believed to occur in the park may appear as a list.

- The classification must be hierarchically organized such that it can be applied at different spatial scales and such that each unit can either be mapped or can be nested uniquely within a single map class.

- The classification must be consistent with the provisions of the National Vegetation Classification Standard (NVCS). It need not use the provisional content of the U.S. National Vegetation Classification (the taxonomy prescribed by the NVCS), but should do so whenever feasible.

- A diagnostic field key to the classified units should be provided. This facilitates identification of the units for purposes of mapping, map validation, accuracy assessment, and applied use of the classification for field applications.

Figure 1 shows the relationship of vegetation classification within the context of other NPS Vegetation Inventory functions for a local (park) project.

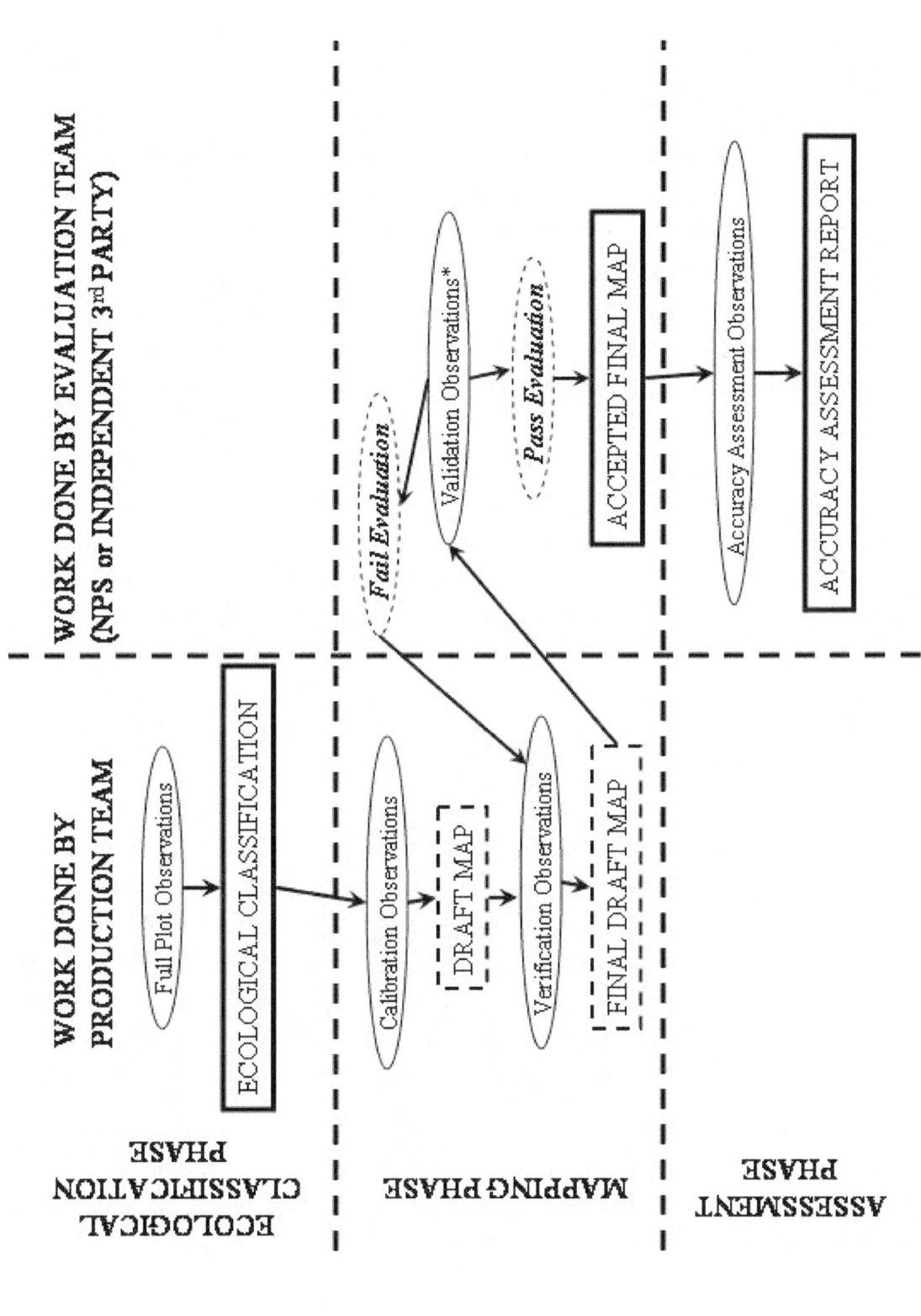

Figure 1. Work Flow of NPS Vegetation Inventory Project. The diagram illustrates the relationship of the field activities for ecological classification, map calibration, map verification, map validation, and thematic accuracy assessment (see http://science.nature.nps.gov/im/inventory/veg.cfm for a full explanation of terms). Items in solid boxes with solid outlines represent products; items in boxes with dashed outlines represent intermediate products; Items in ellipses are field activities. Completion of the ecological classification of vegetation should be an early step in the process.

2.0 Vegetation Classification: Review of Approaches and Methods

2.1 Skills Required and Division of Labor

Investigators (hereafter referred to as classification ecologists) who are considered for vegetation classification should have the following background:

-Understanding of the principles and methods of vegetation community ecology, including appropriate multivariate methods.

-Understanding of vegetation floristic patterns (including knowledge of at least dominant and characteristic species) and probable or potential responses to environmental factors within the study area.

It is desirable that classification ecologists also participate in the collection of classification plot data, which is done prior to the classification. Realistically, many vegetation community ecologists are senior science staff in their organizations who have limited time to spend in the field, and most, if not all, of the plot data collection function often is done by more junior field staff (field ecologists). Field ecologists need good field botany (plant species identification) skills for the project area, but may or may not have a background in vegetation community ecology. The methods of plot data field collection for the NPS Vegetation Inventory can be readily taught to staff with good field botany skills. The plot data collection sampling design to be employed by field ecologists and field data collection methods (see Lea et al. 2011), should be supervised by a classification ecologist. Classification plot data are collected prior to classification.

The classification ecologist creates the classified vegetation units, cross walks them to recognized classification (e.g., to the USNVC) and writes the diagnostic field key. Field ecologists, whose field observation time often provides them with a practical understanding of vegetation patterns, often participate in these functions by writing or assisting in writing vegetation descriptions and by testing field keys.

2.2 Classification Approaches

The classification, or categorization, of natural phenomena, is useful in conservation and natural resource management and inventory in that enables humans to better understand variation (Condit et al. 2011). The objective of any classification is to group together a set of observational units on the basis of their common attributes (Kent and Coker 1992). The end product of a classification should be a set of groups derived from the units of observation whereby units within a group share more attributes with one another than with units in other groups. For vegetation classification, the unit of observation typically is a plot which is representative of, but smaller than, a stand. A stand is a contiguous area of vegetation that is relatively homogeneous in species composition, structure, and ecological setting.

It is beyond the scope and purpose of this document to provide a comprehensive discussion of the many concepts, terms, and methods of vegetation ecology and vegetation community classification. Instead, a few key concepts essential to the program are defined and discussed. A thorough understanding of these concepts is important to the classification function.

Plant species are often viewed as parts of a community of species populations living together in the same area. Mueller-Dombois and Ellenberg (1974) defined a plant community as a: "combination of plants that are dependent on their environment and influence one another and modify their own environment." The classification of plant *communities* yields units with common attributes that are termed *community types* (or vegetation types, or, more simply, types). Communities (or assemblages of plant species) are real and observable biological entities, whereas community types are abstractions of this reality and are models created by humans for practical purposes, such as identification, inventory, and management.

Gleason (1917, 1926), Whittaker (1956, 1962), Curtis (1959), and others held that vegetation units cannot be precisely defined; species comprising a community respond individually to environmental gradients and to each other. The question often became polarized between the "continuum concept" and the "discrete community unit concept" (e.g., Daubenmire 1968, Franklin and Dyrness 1973).

A practical reason for classifying the continuum of vegetation variation into discrete categories (community types) is to simplify the complexity of individual species distributions into relatively few categories that are internally somewhat homogeneous and that can be named and repeatedly identified. Thus, an argument for vegetation classification that transcends the "continuum versus discrete community" controversy can be made: that is, a classification provides means for humans to conceptualize a complex phenomenon and to communicate about it for purposes such as conservation, management, and environmental education. It would be difficult to portray vegetation variation across space on a map as the individualistic response of all species that comprise that vegetation, as opposed to as a relatively few discrete vegetation categories (classes) that are a simplification of the many individual species responses. Conceptual boundaries between classes can be represented as discrete, albeit often arbitrary, dividing lines, and vegetation stands can be modeled in mapping as polygons with definite boundaries. Thus, while the continuum concept indeed may describe the observed reality of vegetation better, a community unit approach is much needed for interpretation and human understanding of this complex reality. While the NPS Vegetation Inventory recognizes the conceptual value of a discrete community model, it must be admitted that the specific "boundaries" of the classes themselves are the most difficult parts of classes to ascertain, for a floristically and ecologically meaningful classification scheme. As rather arbitrary dividing points, they generally make poor starting points for a classification, as is discussed in Subsection 2.2.1. Instead, their position is best approximated by growing the classified units outward from "noda" (core concepts of types), which most vegetation ecologists agree upon as recognizable. The delineation of type boundaries with other types is often done in successive steps as knowledge of the extent of types from the noda grows, and is best done in this manner when the geographic or floristic gradient covered by types and intergrading types is large and not well represented by data.

2.2.1 Vegetation Classification Criteria
The floristic composition of vegetation refers to the combination of individual plant taxa (usually, species) occurring within an individual stand of vegetation or plant community type, along with the absolute or relative abundance of each plant taxon. Quantitative methods of vegetation classification usually heavily rely on floristic composition. A censused list of plant species within a constrained and relatively homogeneous observation area (e.g., a vegetation plot) is a typical and essential part of many vegetation surveys. The abundance of an individual

plant species is often measured as its cover, usually as canopy cover (or absolute canopy cover). The canopy cover of a species (or, where applicable, a group of plant species such as a stratum) is defined as the proportion of ground occupied by the maximum horizontal extent of the vertical projection of the aerial parts of the species (or all species in the group) upon the ground. Individuals or parts of individuals of a species that lie underneath other individuals or parts of that species generally do not add to the species cover. Canopy cover is usually expressed as a percentage, with a maximum cover of any species for a sample unit 100 percent, and the minimum cover zero percent. For classification purposes, the most common practice is ocular estimation of cover over a predetermined plot area in stands in the field. Relative canopy cover is the proportion of all plant (or stratum) canopy cover that is accounted for by an individual species or species group. Relative canopy cover is not estimated in the field, but can be an important derived statistic for classifying, describing, and/or diagnosing vegetation types. Both dominant species and less conspicuous species can be valuable in naming and identifying vegetation community types. Dominant species are often important in mapping the vegetation using remote sensing methods.

The overall appearance of the vegetation is called its physiognomy (Kuchler and Zonneveld 1988). Physiognomy is used to describe the broad features of the vegetation, such as the growth forms and/or the life form of dominant species within a plant community (i.e. trees, shrubs, herbs).

Vegetation structure is defined as the vertical and horizontal size and spacing of the vegetation. Stratification (layering) is the most obvious phenomenon relating to vegetation vertical structure. Examples of strata include tree, shrub, herbaceous, nonvascular, epiphyte, floating, submerged Categorical spacing or density terms (e.g., woodland versus forest) or quantitative modifiers (e.g. percent stratum cover) can be employed to describe horizontal structure.

Understanding the environmental (including biogeographical) setting of vegetation is not required for vegetation classification. However, it is often critical information for the description and inventory (including mapping) of types that have been classified by characteristics (composition, physiognomy, structure) of the vegetation itself. Vegetation types that are placed in different classes from one another based on differences in these vegetation characteristics should also have recognizable differences in environmental setting, or for types that are more influenced by human activities, management history. In other words, environmental and management differences should corroborate and validate putative vegetation differences. General environmental variables that produce variation in vegetation include temperature, moisture, substrate, succession, management history, and competition within and between species. Specific environmental variables include location (geographic setting), elevation, slope, aspect, geologic or soil substrate chemistry and structure, hydrologic regime, and specific disturbance patterns (fire, herbivory, and, for cultural vegetation, human manipulation, etc.).

Thus, a combination of floristic composition, physiognomy, and structure is essential information to identify, classify, and describe plant community types, and data describing these attributes are collected in the field as the basis of a vegetation classification. Environmental, disturbance, and/or management history data are collected as needed to map the vegetation and to provide basic management information about the classified community types.

2.2.2 Noda and Diagnostics

Natural vegetation varies along continuous gradients, but the purpose of classification is to divide these gradients into discrete segments (types) that are homogeneous enough to be readily recognized and understood. Thus, two different, but complementary, aspects of the classification of vegetation should be considered, if the classification is to be applied in a practical manner.

First, the effective description of vegetation requires that common attributes and more typical tendencies of a type be elucidated at some cost of forgoing all possible variations that might best fit within the type. These more typical or central tendencies of the segments are termed "noda" (singular, nodum) (Poore 1956, Lambert and Williams 1962, Roberts 1989). Noda incorporate variation *within* individual vegetation types. Developing a natural classification scheme, such as one that is based strongly on floristic composition, usually is best done using a nodal approach. Indeed, limitations in the ability to make data observations (plots) frequently preclude projects from sampling densely along gradients of variation and force a classification around noda of more closely similar observations as a matter of practical necessity.

In contrast, the identification of features that distinguish the most recognizable conceptual boundaries among individual vegetation types is the diagnosis, and the subset of individual species that are most differential between one type and all other types are termed diagnostic species. By definition, a diagnosis is a *post hoc* activity that follows a classification, rather than guides it, and an effective diagnosis requires that a classification be created first. Nevertheless, the identification of diagnostic species or conditions complements an effective classification by allowing the classified units to be identified individually and/or distinguished from one another.

Good *individual* species that are diagnostic for a vegetation community type tend to have both (1) high fidelity to that type (that is, the species do not occur frequently in other types) and (2) high constancy in that type (that is, they are seldom absent from individual stands of the type). In the practice of vegetation classification, individual plant species that have both of these attributes are not common. This is because highly limited (high fidelity) species tend to be poor competitors and, therefore, are inconstant, even in the type to which they show a high degree of fidelity, whereas constant species are often highly competitive (dominant or otherwise successful species) and so are not limited in distribution.

However, among dominant and/or important species that individually are widely distributed among a number of types, specific combinations and/or combinations of abundances of these species often can provide a reliable diagnosis for a single type. Furthermore, the more thematically coarse a vegetation type is, the less constant individual species will be, and multiple species may be vicariously diagnostic; that is, they may substitute for one another in either presence or abundance in being reliably diagnostic of the type. In the example below from a couplet within a diagnostic field key from Vicksburg National Military Park (Lea et al. in prep.), sweet gum and chinquapin oak are vicariously diagnostic of one vegetation type (and differential between the two types, in the context of this couplet), while water oak and cherrybark oak are vicariously diagnostic of a second vegetation type.

12a. The combined absolute cover of both sweet gum (*Liquidambar styraciflua*) and chinquapin oak (*Quercus muehlenbergii*) is greater than the combined absolute cover of both water oak (*Quercus nigra*) and cherrybark oak (*Quercus pagoda*)...

12

..............................*Liquidambar styraciflua - Carya illinoinensis - Quercus nigra* **Forest**

12b. The combined absolute cover of both sweet gum (*Liquidambar styraciflua*) and chinquapin oak (*Quercus muehlenbergii*) is less than or equal to the combined absolute cover of both water oak (*Quercus nigra*) and cherrybark oak (*Quercus pagoda*)..
....*Quercus pagoda - Quercus nigra* **Forest**

Both noda and diagnostics are important attributes of classified vegetation types that enable recognition of the types in the field and/or from quantitative (plot) data, and both should be given adequate attention if a vegetation classification is to be used successfully for management purposes. Description of typical stands and/or ranges of variation in a type permit recognition of noda as are illustrated in Appendix C. Diagnostic keys are described in Chapter 5 and illustrated in Appendix D.

Figure 2 provides an example of noda and diagnostic boundaries along a limited and relatively simple gradient of vegetation variation. In this example, individual species cover values in vegetation plots collected in the Potomac River fall-line gorge in Maryland, Virginia, and the District of Columbia were plotted against the rank order of 42 vegetation plots along the first axis of a detrended correspondence analysis (DECORANA) Gauch 1982, McCune and Grace 2002) of those plots. This axis also largely corresponds to an environmental gradient of decreasing distance to the river channel, generally decreasing soil depth (from flood scour), and increasing hydroperiod from left to right. Predicted abundances of the individual species were modeled, using a Gaussian regression model, as defined by the equation:

$$ y = A \exp\left[-0.5\left(\frac{x - x_0}{b} \right)^2 \right] $$

where, y is the sample unit abundance value for value x, A is the maximum y (abundance) value in the sample, x is the ordered value of the sample unit on the first DECORANA axis, x_0 is the mean value for x for the sample, and b is the environmental tolerance, as represented by the standard deviation of the x values.

The Gaussian model does not fit all species distributions equally well, but is a reasonable model for purposes of an example, given that many species are unimodal along vegetation and/or environmental gradients that have been comprehensively measured (ter Braak 1996).

As classified by Fleming (2007), the portion of the vegetation gradient portrayed by Nodum A in Figure 2 represents 14 plots classified as the USNVC Potomac River Bedrock Terrace Oak - Hickory Forest, Nodum B represents 10 plots classified as the Appalachian / Northern Piedmont Riverside Outcrop Woodland, Nodum C represents 10 plots classified as the Piedmont / Central Appalachian Riverside Outcrop Prairie, and Nodum D represents eight plots classified as the Fall-line Riverwash Bedrock Prairie.

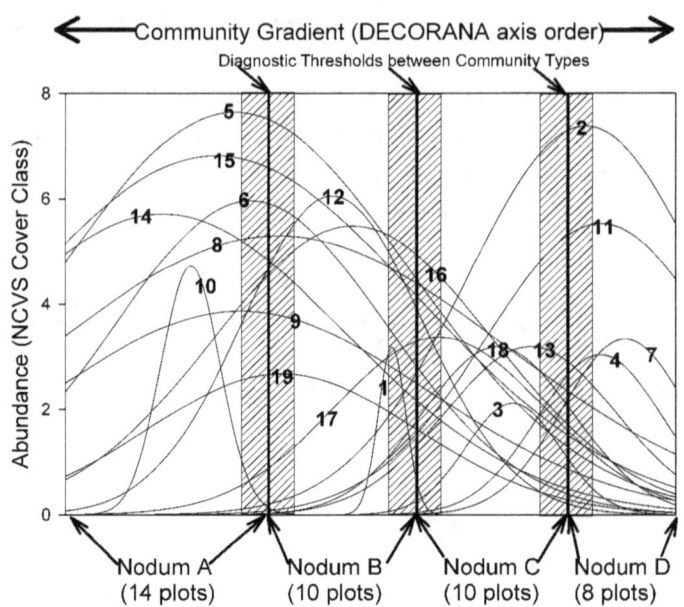

—— 1	*Amelanchier stolonifera*
—— 2	*Andropogon gerardii*
—— 3	*Aristida purpurascens*
—— 4	*Baptisia australis*
—— 5	*Carya glabra*
—— 6	*Danthonia spicata*
—— 7	*Eleocharis compressa*
—— 8	*Fraxinus americana*
—— 9	*Juniperus virginiana*
—— 10	*Melica mutica*
—— 11	*Panicum virgatum*
—— 12	*Pinus virginiana*
—— 13	*Pycnathemum tenuifolium*
—— 14	*Quercus prinus*
—— 15	*Quercus rubra*
—— 16	*Quecus stellata*
—— 17	*Schizachyrium scoparium*
—— 18	*Sorghastrum nutans*
—— 19	*Viburnum rafinesquianum*

Figure 2. Conceptual model of noda and diagnostic boundaries along a vegetation community gradient in the Potomac River fall-line gorge, Maryland, Virginia, and the District of Columbia. The plotted individual curves represent modeled individual species abundance responses in cover class units (methodology from the North Carolina Vegetation Survey of Peet et al. 1998) along a horizontal axis that represents the rank order of 42 individual vegetation plots on river-scoured bedrock features (Lea 2000, Fleming 2007), according to their position along the first axis of a detrended correspondence analysis of the data. The horizontal axis has been partitioned into four classified and intergrading community types (Fleming 2007) that occur along a vegetation compositional gradient from left to right along the axis. Drawn vertical lines perpendicular to the community gradient represent the best idealized "boundaries" between types, while the shaded sections represent transitional parts of the gradient where confusion between types is more likely. An objective of classification is to maximize the horizontal distance occupied by the noda (vegetation types) and to minimize the distance occupied by transitional (shaded) sections by effective identification of diagnostic species.

These noda (or typical expressions) of individual vegetation community types are defined by unique combinations of characteristic individual species (character species), each of which may or may not (and usually do not) have high fidelity to the type. In Figure 2, the curve peaks of species and high relative cover of pignut hickory (*Carya glabra*), northern red oak (*Quercus rubra*), chestnut oak (*Quercus prinus*), poverty oatgrass (*Danthonia spicata*), three-flowered melicgrass (*Melica mutica*), white ash (*Fraxinus americana*), eastern red cedar (*Juniperus virginiana*), and downy arrowwood (*Viburnum rafinesquianum*), largely define the Potomac River Bedrock Terrace Oak - Hickory Forest (Nodum A), with the first five species reaching their maximum abundance in this type (within this gradient). The Appalachian / Northern Piedmont Riverside Outcrop Woodland (Nodum B) is best defined by high relative cover of Virginia pine (*Pinus virginiana*), post oak (*Quercus stellata*), running juneberry (*Amelanchier stolonifera*), pignut hickory (*Carya glabra*), northern red oak (*Quercus rubra*), chestnut oak (*Quercus prinus*), poverty oatgrass (*Danthonia spicata*), white ash (*Fraxinus americana*), eastern red cedar (*Juniperus virginiana*), and downy arrowwood (*Viburnum rafinesquianum*), with the first three species reaching their maximum abundance in this type. The Piedmont / Central Appalachian Riverside Outcrop Prairie (Nodum C) is defined by high relative cover of narrowleaf mountain mint (*Pycnathemum tenuifolium*), little bluestem (*Schizachyrium*

14

scoparium), Indiangrass (*Sorghastrum nutans*), purple three-awn grass (*Aristida purpurascens*), big bluestem (*Andropogon gerardii*), switchgrass (*Panicum virgatum*), post oak (*Quercus stellata*), pignut hickory (*Carya glabra*), northern red oak (*Quercus rubra*), chestnut oak (*Quercus prinus*), poverty oatgrass (*Danthonia spicata*), white ash (*Fraxinus americana*), and eastern red cedar (*Juniperus virginiana*), with the first four species reaching their maximum abundance in this type. The Fall-line Riverwash Bedrock Prairie (Nodum D) is defined by high relative cover of big bluestem (*Andropogon gerardii*), switchgrass (*Panicum virgatum*), Blue false-indigo (*Baptisia australis*), flattened spikerush (*Eleocharis compressa*), and narrowleaf mountain mint (*Pycnathemum tenuifolium*), with the first four species reaching their maximum abundance in this type. As Figure 2 illustrates, none of these character species for the respective types are confined to the type, and most of them are also frequent to abundant in other types.

Of the species examined in this example, the best (though never perfect) *individual* diagnostic species (character species which have high fidelity to, or which are largely confined within, the type of which they are characteristic) can be identified as those species whose distribution is most nearly contained within the nodum of that type. For the four community types addressed here, the best four individual diagnostic species appear to be *Melica mutica, Amelanchier stolonifera, Schizachyrium scoparium*, and *Eleocharis compressa*, respectively. As discussed above, these species are not the most abundant species within the noda of which they are most diagnostic. However, as the individual abundance curve patterns for various species within each nodum also suggest, relatively unique abundance or presence combinations for less restricted species can also serve in the diagnosis of types. For example, a high combined cover of *Pinus virginiana, Quercus stellata*, and *Amelanchier stolonifera* should be *most* characteristic of, the Appalachian / Northern Piedmont Riverside Outcrop Woodland (Nodum B), among these four types, and, therefore, *diagnostic* of that single type, at least within the context of this example.

The continuously varying nature of vegetation means there will almost always be individual vegetation stands (or, in analysis, individual plots) that are ambiguous as to type in any classification scheme. However, because an important classification objective is to increase the usefulness of a classification, the classifier generally attempts to define the conceptual boundaries between vegetation types as narrowly as possible. In Figure 2, this may be conceptualized as decreasing the width of the shaded areas between intergrading types to the width of the narrow lines (i.e., so that more of the transitional plots that represent individual transitional vegetation stands can be assigned to one or another type with confidence with high consistency among different observers).

2.3 Information Sources for Local Vegetation Type Descriptions
As learned from experience, the NPS Vegetation Inventory presently employs a "bottom-up" approach to vegetation classification as a best practice. In this approach, vegetation types are derived from observations (plots) from individual vegetation stands that are grouped and described at the local scale. These locally synthesized groups then are cross walked (as groups, rather than as individual observations) to the best fit in the National Vegetation Classification, for management applications at scales larger than local parks. While a "top-down" approach (e.g., assigning USNVC types to individual plots or observations) may be possible, it has proved to be less effective for local classification and mapping.

Rapp et al. (2005) noted that applying USNVC types to local classification and mapping often necessitated modifications of existing USNVC descriptions and/or additions of types not described by the USNVC. This is because (1) USNVC global type descriptions are sometimes derived from a relatively limited number of sites from across the type's range and some variations are not known to the USNVC, (2) in order to be concise, global descriptions are necessarily homogenized from across a type's range and cannot account for all local variations of the type in a limited amount of text in a description, and (3) some global descriptions are not well defined or described. This situation is expected to improve as the USNVC matures, but a top-down approach likely will prove feasible only when types are well-represented by publicly-accessible plot data that have been formally assigned to types, as prescribed by the NVCS (Federal Geographic Data Committee 2008).

2.3.1 Classification Plots / Local Analysis

Classification plots that are collected from the park site, sometimes supplemented by geographically proximate plots from a more extensive area, serve as a primary source of local floristic and environmental descriptions of vegetation types. Species composition, including abundance or dominance (cover), constancy (frequency among plots), and fidelity can be estimated from the subset of classification plots that have been assigned to that vegetation type. Differences in these values between types can be employed in diagnostic field keys that differentiate types. Values for these measures for a vegetation type are sometimes communicated through synthesis tables of species mean (or median) abundance and constancy by types.

The plot data that have been collected in the field are also used for assigning the vegetation types that have been identified in the park to the corresponding vegetation types within the USNVC that are the best match and for helping to establish diagnostic conditions for mapping. The quantitative plot data also allows for user research and resource management applications beyond the needs for vegetation classification and mapping. For example, frequency of an invasive exotic plant species in plots attributed to a vegetation type may help staff engaged in exotic plant control by allowing them to direct searches for infestations of invasive weeds within that vegetation type in locations where the type has been mapped.

2.3.2 Observation Plots

Observation plots are sample units that collect a more limited set of vegetation and environmental variables than do classification plots. Observation plots are most effectively used when they are collected post-classification, so that the name of a classified vegetation type can be placed on them *a priori* with relatively little new field data collection confidence, including from the use of a diagnostic field key created from data used in developing the classification. Observation plots generally are employed for a broader range of Vegetation Inventory functions than for just the ecological classification; these include mapping functions such as calibration, verification, validation, and thematic accuracy assessment (Figure 1). However, when the floristic data are collected for observation plots, they can both test and refine the ecological classification.

The type and amount of data collected for an observation plot in NPS Vegetation Inventory projects will vary according to the primary function within a project that the plot data are intended to support (Figure 1), as well as according to time and cost considerations (e.g., see Chapter 3 of Lea and Curtis 2010). Minimally, the data recorded for observation plots in NPS projects are (1) a named vegetation type (may be either classified or provisional/*ad hoc*), (2) a geographic position (e.g., northing/easting or latitude/longitude), (3) the date of the observation, (4) the name of the observer(s), and (5) the size of the area actually observed and characterized ("undefined size" is acceptable, if the observation is intended to represent only a characterization of the vegetation at a point at the geographic position and/or if plotless methods are used).

The National Vegetation Classification Standard (NVCS) defines "occurrence plots" as plots that are collected for documenting the occurrence of a previously defined vegetation type (Federal Geographic Data Committee 2008). Minimum data requirements for NVCS occurrence plots include all of those that are specified for NPS observation plots (above), plus names of the dominant plant taxa and their cover values (or other measure of abundance). Depending on the data collected, some NPS observation plots will meet the requirements, while others may not. However, many observation plots that would not meet the FGDC conditions for an occurrence plot still would document types and their locations adequately in the context of a local classification, and, often, in the context of the NVCS. This is because vegetation types identified in observation plots in NPS projects are usually derived from a rigorous quantitative analysis of local classification plots and/or from locally specific diagnostic field keys derived from that analysis. These are advantages that are seldom available for global circumscriptions of USNVC types. Therefore, the amount of data collected for NPS observation plots should not be governed by the requirements of NVCS occurrence plots, but by the costs and benefits of their application to local project tasks. Lea and Curtis (2010) give examples of various amounts of reference data that may be collected for observation plots that are used for thematic accuracy assessment, depending on the balance between cost and reference data accuracy needed.

Those observation plots that do collect floristic and species abundance data may, in turn, provide data to help refine the classification.

2.3.3 Remotely Sensed Image Data

Because vegetation mapping in the NPS Vegetation Inventory should follow an *a priori* vegetation classification that is based on floristic and ecological data that have been observed in the field, mapping criteria should not be used to develop central concepts (noda) of vegetation types. However, mapping criteria that make sense for a particular site may be used to refine the differential criteria (conceptual boundaries) between individual intergrading types, especially when ecological investigation suggests that those criteria are a single variable that varies along a continuum, such as abundance (cover) of a dominant species that can be identified from a remotely sensed image. While a perspective of vegetation from a remotely sensed image cannot detect fine-scale attributes of stands, it does allow the observation of many more stands than usually can be observed in the field, so that more observations of coarse-scale attributes can be made. For example, the difference between the Southern Rocky Mountain Ponderosa Pine Savanna (USNVC Group G229) and the floristically similar and intergrading Southern Rocky Mountain Montane-Subalpine Grassland (USNVC Group G268) may be primarily the level of abundance (as measured by canopy cover) of ponderosa pine (*Pinus ponderosa*) in stands, at both field and at remotely sensed observation scales. Field observations that estimate ponderosa pine cover may not include enough transitional stands between the savanna type and the grassland type to establish precise differential ponderosa pine cover values that would allow consistent distinction between sparsely wooded stands of the savanna type and stands of the grassland type that have some scattered trees. By observing transitional patterns from one type to the other across many stands, a mapper can find logical and repeatable mapping criteria between the two types. By sampling (on the image) ponderosa pine cover of a of reasonably large number of transitional stands of both types (preferably at the scale of the minimum mapping unit for the types), the mapper can estimate a more precise differential (threshold) value for ponderosa pine cover than might be obtained from a limited number of field observations. The differential value derived from the remotely sensed perspective would likely serve as the best local differentiation (boundary) between the two types for the field-based classification, if field observations do not cover the full range of physiognomic variability of both types, or if a generalized classification scheme (e.g., the USNVC) that is not yet based on range wide quantitative analyses offers estimated differential thresholds that do not apply well to the local area or to some types.

As another example, a mapping project in the Sierra Nevada foothills of California may encounter grasslands comprised primarily of annual grass species as one vegetation type and woodlands of blue oak (*Quercus douglassi*) over the same assemblage of annual grasses. The two types may intergrade with each other in a mosaic pattern over large areas. Except for the greater abundance of blue oak in the latter type, floristic differences between the two types may be nearly indiscernible, and plot data collected from the two types may show a wide gap in the abundance of the primary differential species (e.g., 1% for the highest blue oak cover in any grassland plot and 25% for the lowest blue oak cover in any blue oak woodland plot). Global descriptions (e.g., from the USNVC) may identify a cover criteria of 10% cover or more of blue oak for the woodland type as the primary differentiating condition, but mappers may observe that a large proportion of stands have near 10% blue oak cover, making it difficult to differentiate between the types for many intergrading stands by this rule and rendering the accuracy of a diagnosis overly arbitrary and highly dependent on observation area size. From density patterns of blue oak over large areas, the mappers may observe that using 7% blue oak cover as a differential threshold between the blue oak woodland type and the annual grass herbaceous type yields fewer stands that are transitional and difficult to differentiate or diagnose, either from mapping or in the field.

In such a case, it would be acceptable to accept a differential or diagnostic criterion of 7% blue oak cover as for recognizing blue oak woodlands from annual grasslands and/or other non-wooded types, recognizing that a cover abundance for blue oak of 7% or more is within an acceptable range of between-site variation for a differential criterion that may average 10% globally.

This recommendation does not advocate using remotely sensed criteria to *determine the vegetation types*; rather, it allows the remote sensing and mapping processes to *reasonably influence the diagnoses (thresholds)* for vegetation types that are more clearly established *a priori* from ecological field observations and analysis. It is based on the recognition that distinctions between types may vary from site to site, that local plot data may not sufficiently intensive to establish precise differential thresholds in dominant species cover, and that specific and reliable differential criteria conditions may not be available at the scale of the USNVC.

2.3.4 Regional Classification Plots / Regional Analysis

In a limited number of situations, reasonably comprehensive plot data across the range of some vegetation types that are addressed in an individual NPS park project may exist and can be readily incorporated into an analysis that provides descriptions that are precise enough for local mapping and management. In these cases, the global description may be used in lieu of a local (park-specific) description, or the local description may be created from minor editing of the global description (e.g., deleting names of plant taxa that may be typical of a type throughout most of its range, but that do not occur in or are atypical of the type within the local (park) stands).

2.4 Information Sources for Global (National Vegetation Classification) Description

2.4.1 Classification Plots / USNVC Types Database

NatureServe Explorer (NatureServe 2009) is a web application that is a public portal into NatureServe's database of vegetation community types, which, as of this writing, serves the function of the USNVC types database until a federally guided version (Federal Geographic Data Committee 2008) can be implemented. Global (range wide) information about USNVC associations and alliances is available for adding to reports, as needed. NPS project reports should be sure to properly follow the citation guidelines and credit NatureServe (2009). These citation guidelines can be found at the bottom of pages representing individual Association or Alliance descriptions.

Although the search capabilities of NatureServe Explorer are somewhat limited at the time of this guidance, fairly thorough searches can be accomplished with practice and familiarity. Generally, the most effective means of searching for a potential USNVC type match to a local vegetation type is to search based on one or more characteristic or dominant plant species of the local type, perhaps constraining the search to the states or ecoregions of and around the local site.

It should be noted that the taxonomic and descriptive content of NatureServe Explorer is considered provisional in terms of the NVCS (Federal Geographic Data Committee 2008) and that not all vegetation types are well defined. In particular, seminatural (including ruderal or weedy) vegetation is not well represented. In cases where a type found in a NPS project appears not to correspond, even partially, to any known USNVC type, a NPS provisional name may be assigned (see Subsection 4.1.1). Documenting these types not only defines them for purposes of the local project, but also allows for subsequent review for possible eventual incorporation into the USNVC.

At the time of this publication, vegetation types that are documented on NatureServe Explorer are organized by the 1997 NVCS hierarchy (FGDC 1997). A first approximation of descriptions for types of the USNVC middle level group (see Table 1, Appendix A) and their relationships to existing Associations was sponsored by a cooperative effort of the National Park Service and LANDFIRE (http://www.landfire.gov) and conducted by NatureServe and a number of USNVC development partners from 2008 to 2011 (Faber-Langendoen et al. 2010). Additionally, as of 2011, the Hierarchy Revisions Working Group of the FGDC Vegetation Subcommittee has initiated descriptions of units of the USNVC upper level of class (Table 1). Following peer review of these descriptions by the Ecological Society of America Panel on Vegetation

Classification (http://www.esa.org/vegweb/), it is anticipated that the descriptions will be available at http://usnvc.org in late 2011, with periodic updates.

2.5 Review of Quantitative Methods for Vegetation Classification

The creation of a complete set of descriptions and diagnoses of local vegetation types is based on both the plot data collected in the field during this project and other suitable existing vegetation information. Floristic patterns comprising these types and their general relationship to key environmental variables in the park are identified either quantitatively using analysis programs or qualitatively (see Grossman et al. (1998), pp. 35-36 for an overview of the latter process).

The recognition of the distribution patterns of vegetation along environmental gradients that can be detected using remotely sensed or derived data will facilitate vegetation mapping and subsequent management of the parks resources. Because plot data collected at each site contain both environmental and vegetation information of the sampled plant community and precise site location is recorded, trends in the relationship between the vegetation and the environment can be identified, although additional post-classification observations of the type are often needed to detect these trends.

As a general rule, an analysis that groups individual sample units (plots) into relatively homogeneous groups (local types), followed by a cross walking of these groups to an established classification scheme (e.g., the USNVC) will yield more robust results than will an attempt to cross walk or classify individual sample units without regard to their local group membership. This is because individual plots will not contain all elements of a stand, and individual, geographically restricted stands will not contain all elements of a type. This does not preclude the possibility that, in analysis, some individual sample units may form their own group (outliers) and also may be distinct enough within the local data set and when compared to the USNVC that cross walking is possible from a single sample unit.

2.5.1 Cluster Analysis

Cluster analysis is the most commonly employed and, often, the most robust, method of grouping sample units in order to produce a natural (multivariate) classification scheme. Cluster analysis is agglomerative ("bottom up") with regard to the individual sample unit. It requires choices of distance (dissimilarity) measures (to establish inter-sample unit differences in individual dimensions) and in linkage methods (grouping algorithms). These choices will affect the grouping and interpretability of the results; the best choices may depend on the nature of the data themselves. A product of cluster analysis in almost all statistical packages (e.g., McCune and Mefford 1999) is a dendrogram, which shows visual representation of the clustering hierarchy. Hierarchical clustering *per se* cannot determine at what level of the hierarchy clusters should be recognized as types. This question may be resolved by subjective interpretation of the groups or by objective measures that test the validity of the groups. McCune and Grace (2002) provide a review of clustering analysis and of testing groupings produced by any classification method.

2.5.2 TWINSPAN

TWINSPAN (Two-way Indicator Species Analysis) (Hill 1979, Gauch and Whittaker 1981, McCune and Grace 2002) is a grouping method that differs from cluster analysis in that it is a divisive ("top-down") approach that begins with the entire sample, rather than with the individual sample unit. It creates groups by employing an ordination method, correspondence analysis (reciprocal averaging) to create the progressive dichotomous divisions in the sample (McCune and Grace 2002).

The relative frequency of the use of TWINSPAN for vegetation classification likely has declined in recent years because of the limitations inherent in its parent ordination method in representing ecological data that reflect a response to more than one important gradient (e.g., floristic gradients that are responding to large changes in both elevation and substrate chemistry simultaneously and orthogonally (in a weakly correlated or non-correlated manner). This situation might occur in a large data set from a large and ecologically complex park, especially where multiple significant environmental factors are known to have major effects on vegetation. The use of TWINSPAN in this situation may create groupings that are less interpretable than are those produced by cluster analysis using the same data. Nevertheless, TWINSPAN often yields results that compare well to cluster analysis when response gradients are fairly simple, such as less heterogeneous data sets. These less heterogeneous data sets may be subsets of a larger data set, in which the sample units are believed to be responding to only one major environmental/floristic gradient. Furthermore, the ordered species by sample units table produced by TWINSPAN is quite appealing as a means to understand indicator (diagnostic) species patterns, as long as one trusts the groupings.

2.5.3 Tabular Sorting
This family of methods (Mueller-Dombois and Ellenberg 1974) is primarily subjective and dates at least to the early 20th century. While they can be used as a primary classification means, their use in even modestly large and heterogeneous data sets would be difficult. Their best use in all but the smallest data sets is probably as a *post hoc* refinement of individual sample unit (plot) memberships within groupings that are derived from a more objective and efficient grouping method (e.g., cluster analysis).

Two common means of sorting are used. First, sample units may be ordered into progressively more similar groups within vegetation plot table (e.g., in a spreadsheet software program), based on previously calculated inter-sample unit measures of similarity or distance (dissimilarity) that have been entered into the individual table cells that represent each pair of compared plots. Positions of individual plots within the array of rows and columns are manually moved to bring cells with high similarity (or low dissimilarity) values close together in order in the table. This process is more efficient when used as a refinement of another classification method whereby the initial position of the sample units in the table is in groups produced by the other classification method. High inter-group similarities may identify groups that are too finely split by the original classification; conversely low within-group similarities may indicate too "lumped" a treatment. While Mueller Dombois and Ellenberg (1974) suggested that absolute levels of similarity between sample units might guide recognition of types, there is evidence that elements of sample unit diversity (species richness and/or species evenness) may influence mathematical similarity between sample units relative to the recognizable ecological similarity between the vegetation stands that they represent. Therefore, the application of similarity thresholds for determining groups should be applied as a relative, rather than an absolute, guide.

As a second method, a species by sample unit table may be used to reclassify individual sample units subjectively. This tends to be tedious if the data set is moderately large and also requires a thorough understanding of the site. A more common modern use of such a table is to generate summary statistics on individual species (e.g., constancy, mean abundance), sometimes called synthesis tables, from classified groups of sample units in order to develop diagnostic criteria, as when constructing a field key. Some sorting pursuant to this may improve the description and identification of classified types by giving higher diagnostic values in some species.

The freeware program JUICE 7.0 (Tichy 2002, Tichy and Holt 2006) (http://www.sci.muni.cz/botany/juice/index.htm.) is useful for sorting and reassigning sample units into groups. Spreadsheet programs may also be used.

2.5.4 Indicator Species Analysis
Indicator Species Analysis (Dufrêne, M. and P. Legendre 1997, McCune and Grace 2002) is not a classification method *per se*, but it is mentioned here because it is sometimes claimed to serve that role (it would be extremely tedious to attempt it). Rather it a useful *post hoc* means of developing indicator or diagnostic species for type identification, as in a field key, but the method requires that groups first be defined using a different method (either qualitative or quantitative).

2.5.5 Ordination
Ordination methods *per se* do not classify (produce groupings). They place and display individual variables, including either sample units (plots) or species along axes in multi-dimensional space that are scaled to differences between the sample units, so that the relative differences and similarities between individual sample units or other variables (species) are elucidated. Thus, ordination methods maintain some complexity (less reduction of multivariate data) in order to allow [often graphical] insight into the relative positioning of sample units along more than one significant gradient and to generate hypotheses about causes. Ordination is not required for classification, but is mentioned here because of its common complementary or supplementary use in many classification studies. Some ordination algorithms combine ordination and classification objectives by also deriving and showing suggested groupings of sample units based on their distance from one another, while retaining their individual position relative to other units. Common ordination methods include nonmetric multidimensional scaling (NMDS) (Kruskal 1964), principle components analysis (PCA) (Pielou 1984), Detrended Correspondence Analysis (DCA) (Hill and Gauch 1980), and canonical correspondence analysis (CCA) (ter Braak 1990). The first method is representative of a group of ordination techniques that emphasize inter-sample unit distance, while the three latter methods emphasize the order of individual species order along multiple axes in ordination space, as derived from eigenanalysis. McCune and Grace (2002) present a review of several common methods.

3.0 Vegetation Classification: Relationship to Map Classes

Experience in applying vegetation classification to resource management and research within the NPS Vegetation Inventory has shown that the classification and description of vegetation from a field perspective alone seldom is sufficient for resource management and stewardship activities. Resource management staff and researchers usually have limited time to conduct site visits and also may not have the botanical skills to assess vegetation in the field. Thus, much vegetation management within the NPS and other land management agencies must be planned and conducted remotely and, therefore, relies on spatially explicit and spatially precise models of the vegetation (i.e., vegetation maps). Map classes that are well described, ecologically based, and mapped with reasonable accuracy are critical in ensuring that an ecologically meaningful vegetation classification is employed in management and research. Therefore, it is important that vegetation classification and vegetation mapping be well integrated, so that map classes either (1) represent well-described vegetation classes in a 1:1 relationship or (2), where this is not possible, that map classes be explicitly related to described ecological classes in an explicit one-to-many, strictly hierarchical relationship (i.e., each vegetation class is a member of only one map class). In infrequent cases, a vegetation class may be represented by more than one map class (e.g., different expressions of a single vegetation type that are important to distinguish and can also easily be distinguished from each other using remotely sensed data). In these cases, the map class to vegetation class relationship also should be hierarchical, and each map class should represent only that single vegetation type. "In part" relationships between map classes and vegetation classes should be avoided (and can be, with good planning) because they create unnecessary complexities and ambiguities in analyses of vegetation types are made from map classes.

3.1 Vegetation and Unvegetated Land Cover That Are Represented by Single (Homogeneous) Map Classes

3.1.1 Natural and Seminatural Vegetation
Natural vegetation includes vegetation whose floristic composition and vegetation structure has been little affected by human activities. It also is represented by vegetation that may have been more profoundly affected by human activities, but has recovered to the point at which the effects are insignificant for purposes of a floristic classification (e.g., many secondary forests on formerly cleared land after 50 to 100 years of recovery). It is often useful to define natural vegetation as all land cover that does not meet seminatural, cultural, or unvegetated land cover criteria.

Seminatural vegetation includes anthropogenic vegetation whose composition, physiognomy and/or structure show significant effects from past human activities, but is not currently subjected to significant intentional and periodic manipulation by humans. Since most vegetation in the United States has been modified by humans, either directly (e.g., agriculture, forestry) or indirectly (e.g., unintentional introduction of invasive non-native plant species or tree pathogens), the distinction between natural and seminatural can be obscure. The term "seminatural" generally is used to describe stands in which the anthropogenic influence creates a clear floristic distinction from the composition of fully natural stands. Seminatural vegetation types often are described as "ruderal" or "weedy." It includes forests dominated by early successional tree species that occupy a recently clearcut, old fields developing from formerly

23

farmed areas, and vegetation stands dominated by invasive non-native species. Although forest plantations (even those dominated by planted non-native species) require periodic human activity in order to persist, they are treated by the USNVC as seminatural, rather than cultural, vegetation because the long time span between human interventions often allow natural processes to introduce native components, which makes plantations floristically very similar to seminatural successional stands.

In an ecological context, environmental influences on existing seminatural vegetation that follow anthropogenic disturbance are essentially the same as for fully natural vegetation, and the predominance of these factors over active anthropogenic management unites natural and seminatural vegetation types and distinguishes them from cultural vegetation types. In the United States, seminatural vegetation types often have received lesser conservation and research interest than types assessed to be more natural. For this reason, seminatural types are often less well described and are classified more broadly and using more technical criteria (e.g., individual stand dominance by a single species) than are related fully natural types. Due to the uncertainty associated with classification of seminatural USNVC types, global information on these types is maintained, but not currently served publicly, by NatureServe (NatureServe 2009). In addition, a number of seminatural vegetation types that will be encountered in parks are not yet recognized by the USNVC and will need to be named and described from local observation only.

3.1.3 Cultural Vegetation
Cultural vegetation, equivalent to planted/cultivated vegetation of the 1997 NVCS (Federal Geographic Data Committee 1997), includes anthropogenic vegetation that requires periodic intervention by human activities (mowing, agriculture, clearing, horticulture, etc.) in order to persist. Anthropogenic vegetation types include vegetation of lawns, athletic fields, gardens, orchards, agricultural fields, arboreta, and landscaped areas. The NPS Vegetation Inventory currently uses the vegetation classes of Levels 1 through 6 of the pilot example (Appendix I) of the Federal Geographic Data Committee (2008) to define cultural vegetation types.

3.1.4 Unvegetated Land (and Water) Cover and Some Problematic Vegetation Classes
While a mapping project that is focused on vegetation might simply eliminate land cover that is truly unvegetated, the needs of vegetation and land cover applications often closely overlap, so that the mapping component of the NPS Vegetation Inventory should include [truly] unvegetated land cover, wherever an applicable vegetation class cannot be applied. Unvegetated land cover includes two major categories. The first represents anthropogenic surfaces that have been so modified as to exclude plant growth or to limit plant growth to inconsequential abundance (e.g., pavement, buildings, active quarries). The second category represents natural surfaces that never support macroscopic vegetation (e.g., open water, seasonally permanent snow or ice, extremely active sand dunes, intertidal zones with unstable substrates (e.g., sand), and infrequently exposed parts of river channels and playas.

Most natural rock surfaces (e.g., outcrops, talus) have a significant nonvascular (especially lichen) vegetation component and are included as natural vegetation in the USNVC. Similarly, surfaces dominated by an ephemeral vascular plant component that can be of sparse and/or irregular cover, but is floristically predictable (e.g., coastal shore vegetation, playa vegetation, desert pavement vegetation, scree vegetation, some sand dune vegetation) should be treated as natural vegetation. Challenges of taxonomic identification of community component taxa (e.g., non vascular species) or of phenological timing of observations may preclude the creation of specific and thorough local floristic description of these vegetation types or their placement at lower levels within the USNVC. In these cases, the types should be described as much as the observation timing and taxonomic expertise will allow and cross walked into the lowest levels of the USNVC as possible.

Ultimately, areas that are mapped as unvegetated "Open Water" may be classified and mapped by their benthic substrate component. Local classification of marine, estuarine, and major lacustrine systems is being addressed by a different NPS natural resources inventory effort (Moses et al. 2010). National classification standards in these ecological areas are being addressed by the Federal Geographic Data Committee and partners and are more recent developments than the USNVC (see http://www.fgdc.gov/standards/projects/FGDC-standards-projects/cmecs-folder/cmecs-index-page). These classifications may overlap with the USNVC for submerged aquatic and some emergent or intertidal macrophyte vegetation. Ultimately, all fresh water (including riverine and smaller lacustrine) non-vegetated ecological systems may be included. Addressing the possible coordination of vegetation and aquatic mapping is mentioned here for future consideration, but is beyond the scope of the current NPS Vegetation Inventory activities.

3.2 Heterogeneous Map Classes (Complexes)
Multiple vegetation types that tend to occur together in a landscape have been referred to as vegetation complexes (Mueller-Dombois and Ellenberg 1974). Often, these vegetation types can be discerned individually on the ground, but cannot be distinguished from one another in mapping from remotely sensed data. They often occur in stands that typically are smaller than the defined minimum mapping unit for a vegetation mapping project. These complexes are most often wetland types arranged along a steep hydrological gradient (i.e., a relatively large hydroperiod change over a relatively short horizontal distance) in an either unidirectional or less predictable succession. They include patterned bogs or fens, vernal pools, marshes, floodplains, riparian and lacustrine shorelines. In these situations, the multiple indistinguishable types may force a practical mapping aggregation to form a many-to-one relationship with a recognized vegetation type at a higher hierarchy level in the selected classification (e.g., the USNVC). The map class name may reflect this relationship or the units may aggregate at such a high level in the hierarchy that a local class name may be more appropriate. In either case, the relationship between the thematically finest map class and the vegetation types should be made explicit, preferably as a relationship within the spatial database itself (e.g., by means of a "look-up" table). The map class should also be cross walked to the lowest level of the USNVC hierarchy that accommodates all ecological classes denoted by the map class. A map class may be given a local (project-specific) name and a standard (USNVC) name simply by creating two database fields, allowing for use of the data at multiple scales.

3.2.1 Thematic Complexes
In some cases, more than one distinct vegetation type may occur in repeating patches that are each consistently larger than the minimum mapping unit, but are so floristically, geographically, and environmentally similar as to be not consistently indistinguishable from remotely sensed data. In these cases, the similarities causing these mapping challenges can also make the types difficult to distinguish on the ground.

As opposed to the case of spatial confusion or mosaicing, in which ecological classes are easily diagnosed on the ground from floristic and fine-scale environmental patterns, but simply occur in stands too small to discern from remotely sensed data (see next subsection), thematic similarities not related to remotely sensed data limitations should prompt ecologists to consider whether the types might better be treated as a single ecological class, at least at the local scale, in view of the fact that local floristic field data also might fail to diagnose them well.

If it is determined that the purported multiple types can be readily diagnosed by a ground observer, but simply cannot be differentiated from a remote sensing perspective, then the map class may be mapped as a *thematic complex* of the types. A complex of thematically fine types may be equivalent to thematically coarser classes in a hierarchical vegetation classification or may be an *ad hoc* grouping (Rapp et al. 2005).

3.2.2 Mosaiced Complexes
In some cases, more than one distinct vegetation type can occur together in repeating patches. The typical area occupied by each of the individual types may be smaller than the minimum mapping unit for a project, but the patches of the combined types typically may exceed the minimum mapping unit and are ecologically and/or spatially related. The individual types either may be indiscernible to the mapper at all, or they may be evident as individual types that are intermixed with one another to a degree that would make it overly complex and inefficient to map them as individual stands. These situations occur most frequently, but not exclusively, in riparian or wetland vegetation (e.g., patterned fens, riparian bars, zoned edges of vernal pools). In these cases, the components are recognized as different vegetation types for purposes of vegetation classification and description, but since the patches of each component are less than the minimum mapping unit, they are treated as a single map class comprised of both vegetation types.

The mosaiced complex map class might be equivalent to a recognized USNVC unit at a higher level in the USNVC hierarchy than the individual types that comprise it. In this case, a spatial database field may crosswalk the map class to the higher USNVC level, and a local map class can specify that it is a combination of specific lower level units (i.e., it does not contain all USNVC lower level units that comprise in the high level unit on a global scale).

3.4 Cross Walk of Local Vegetation Classes to National Vegetation Classification
At the time of this guidance, the organization and public serving of USNVC content data is transitional from NatureServe to the federal sector. Descriptions of the newly defined upper and middle levels of the USNVC (class through group, see Appendix A, including Table 1) are available at http://www.usnvc.org. Descriptions of the lower (thematically finest) of the USNVC (Alliances and Associations) but [currently] not their placement in the 2008 USNVC hierarchy, are available at http://www.natureserve.org/explorer.

3.5 Cross Walk of Local Vegetation Classes to Local Map Classes
Ideally, the primary map classes will be the same as vegetation classes (i.e., a 1:1 relationship). Where this is not possible, map classes and vegetation classes will be in a non-overlapping one-to-many hierarchy (with occasional many-to-one exceptions). This means that individual vegetation classes should not be represented as having an "in part" relationship with any map class.

3.6 Cross Walk to Other Classifications

It may be useful to classify vegetation types that are identified during NPS Vegetation Inventory projects to other classifications, including local (including state) classifications, wetland classifications (e.g., Cowardin et al. 1979), land cover classifications, and national mapping classifications, including NatureServe's Ecological Systems (Comer et al. 2003). Many of these classification schemes are not strictly hierarchical or are only partially hierarchical with respect to the USNVC on a comprehensive (global or national) scale (e.g., Comer et al. 2003; Cowardin et al. 1979). However, they often may work in a strictly hierarchical manner on a local (park) scale and, therefore, suffice for requirements of this guidance. For example, on a national (global) scale, the USNVC Association known as the Broadleaf Cattail Marsh (= *Typha (latifolia, angustifolia)* Western Herbaceous Vegetation) has membership in both the Western Great Plains Open Freshwater Depression Wetland Ecological System and the Western Great Plains Floodplain Ecological System of Comer et al. (2003). If this global relationship between the Ecological Systems and the association also were the case at the park scale, then these Ecological Systems would be unsuitable as a map class because, in this case, a thematically finer vegetation type recognized in the park is not hierarchical within them and occurs in more than one. However, if (1) only one of these Ecological Systems is present in the park or (2) if both Ecological Systems are present, but the Broadleaf Cattail Marsh is known to occur in and is represented to occur in only one of them at the park scale, then these Systems are suitable map classes for the park project. In other words, cross walks should be made on the vegetation type scale (for which the cross walks can be made as a database field aggregation or cross walk), rather than at an individual stand scale (which would require additional mapping effort).

3.7 Representation within Spatial Database

It is generally preferable to represent these cross walks as additional database fields in the spatial (Geographic Information System) database that represents the map classes. While a park map class field may include units from more than one classification system, each hierarchical level within each classification system used to describe map classes (e.g., each hierarchy level of the USNVC, each hierarchy level of the National Land Cover Data, state classification, Ecological Systems, local (park) attributes, etc.) should have a dedicated field in the spatial database that contains only units and names used within that system and level. This is necessary if there is a need to aggregate units between projects or to create legends of varying thematic resolution for different map users. The use of look-up tables in a relational database will facilitate this need.

4.0 Vegetation Descriptions

4.1 Minimum Requirements

Each vegetation type that occurs in the park should be well described as it can be observed in the park, drawing on the plot data and other observations collected in the park (a local description). Whenever a vegetation type can be attributed to a U.S. National Vegetation Classification (USNVC) vegetation type concept and a more geographically extensive description is available at the time of the project (e.g., NatureServe 2009), the type description may include existing information from across the entire range of the type's distribution (e.g., a national or global description). Where a type that is clearly unique within the project area is not recognized or described by the USNVC database, the type may be designated as a NPS provisional type, with no global description provided in the classification report.

New work on development of only vegetation type descriptions will be funded only at a single geographic scale (global or local) and only a single hierarchy level for each NPS Vegetation Inventory project. Normally, the geographic scale will be local because of the need to apply the classification to local mapping and local resource management and because access to global descriptions is currently limited. Improvements to global information will be limited to editing errors and increasing range distribution (or incorporating the local description as the global description for types discovered in NPS projects).

In some cases, reasonably comprehensive plot data across the range of some vegetation types that are identified in the NPS park project exist and can be readily incorporated into an analysis. In these cases, a regional/global scale analysis and type circumscription development or modification may be substituted for the park scale analysis and type description work. The global description then should be adequate for the local needs, or the local description can be created from minor editing of the global description (e.g., deleting names of plant taxa that may be typical of a type throughout most of its range, but that do not occur in or are atypical of the type within the local (park) stands).

4.1.1 Minimum Set of Fields for Vegetation Type Descriptions

The following sets of fields should be included in all vegetation type descriptions created for parks by the NPS Vegetation Inventory.

- Local name (this may be the same as the USNVC name).

- Unique Identifier (USNVC or NPS). If the vegetation type is a recognized USNVC type, the identifier currently assigned by NatureServe (NatureServe 2009) is used (association identifiers are alphanumeric and begin with "CEGL00;" alliance identifiers begin with "A."). For types developed by the project (NPS provisional types), the identifier will be a ten digit alphanumeric code, with the first three Digits "NPS," the next four digits the acronym of the park, and the last three digits a consecutive number, starting with "001." Thus, the first NPS provisional type for Little Bighorn Battlefield National Monument (LIBI) will be "NPSLIBI001;" the second provisional type for that unit will be designated as "NPSLIBI002" (see Appendix C, Exhibit 2).

- USNVC Name (if available) from NatureServe 2009) (include Latin Names for Alliance and Association).

- USNVC Hierarchy Placement (currently, from http://usnvc.org).

- Local Floristic Description (from project data).

- Local Environmental Description (from project data).

- Local Map Class That Represents or Contains Type (from project data).

4.1.2 Optional Set of Fields for Vegetation Type Descriptions

The following sets of fields may be included in vegetation type descriptions created for parks by the NPS Vegetation Inventory.

- Local (Park) Distribution (from project data).

- Global Distribution (Range) (from NatureServe 2009).

- Other Classification Cross Walk: e.g., Wetland (Cowardin et al. (1979), NatureServe Ecological Systems (Comer et al. 2003), State Classifications.

- Global Floristic Description (from NatureServe 2009).

- Global Environmental Description (from NatureServe 2009).

- List of Local Field Plots that have been Assigned to the Type.

- List of Local Dominant and/or Characteristic Species of Type.

- Global Conservation Rank (from NatureServe 2009).

- Local Plot Synthesis Table.

- Local and/or Global Comments.

- Local and/or Global Scientific Name Translated to English

- Local and/or Global Classification Confidence Level.

- Other Noteworthy Local Species known from the Type.

- References

4.2 Sources for Description

4.2.1 Classification Plots

Classification plot data are the primary source of information for constructing a local description for a vegetation type recognized by a project. From the set of plots that have been classified as a type, the constancy, mean abundances, and ranges of abundances of plant species within a vegetation type may be calculated as a synthesis table. These metrics provide quantitative characteristics of a type. Environmental and geographic data collected with the plots provide information about the type's expected occurrence within the park.

4.2.2 Observation Plots
Observation plots used for developing a mapping model or for validating or assessing the accuracy of a map may include additional floristic and environmental information from more stands. Since classification and description normally precedes mapping and assessment, this information will often be added during and/or following the mapping phase in order to improve the local description.

4.2.3 USNVC Types Database
When a type can be cross walked (matched to) a recognized USNVC type, information from the USNVC database (currently NatureServe 2009) may be incorporated to provide a larger regional context to the local description. Often, floristic composition of a vegetation type observed within a park may differ somewhat from a global description and/or the global characteristics of the type may be poorly known or incomplete. Nominal species in the global name may not fit local (park) stands optimally.

4.2.4 Map Data
Classification descriptions will be completed prior to mapping (Figure 1). However, if post-classification activities, including mapping and accuracy assessment provide useful additional information, such as differential information (see Subsection 2.3.3) or a better understanding of a type's distribution within the park, this information may be appended to the description and/or field key.

4.2.5 Qualitative Sources
Informal observations and notes on stands of a type may further contribute to the descriptions.

5.0 Field Keys

5.1 Purposes of Field Keys

Field keys to vegetation are a hierarchical set of steps of two or more alternative and contrasting statements about vegetation conditions. At each step, the key user reads each alternative statement and observes characteristics of the vegetation that enable the best (most true) alternative statement to be selected. Each alternative selected leads the user to another set of alternatives or to a named vegetation type. The user progresses through each step until a vegetation type is arrived at, as most probable answer. Each individual step represents a *differentiation* between two sets of vegetation type; the entire process results in a *diagnosis* of a vegetation type (i.e., a differentiation of that type from all other possible types).

Field keys are a useful means for rapidly and objectively identifying (diagnosing) vegetation stands *in situ* for purposes of research, inventory, monitoring, and management. While they are never a complete substitute for more detailed descriptions of vegetation types and/or experience with vegetation, they help to allow competent non-experts the means to reliably diagnose vegetation types in the absence of experience with the types. In turn, they promote the broader use of vegetation classification beyond the realm of vegetation classification experts.

In the NPS Vegetation Inventory, field keys to the vegetation types are developed on a park-by-park basis. These keys should be based on the local vegetation classification and designed to allow the diagnosis of any vegetation type that may be encountered in the field (whether mapped individually or as a part of a map complex). Since the vegetation classes must be nested hierarchically and uniquely within map classes, when not equivalent to an individual map class, the vegetation type key may be used to validate and assess the accuracy of the vegetation map because the keyed vegetation type will determine the map class by its declared membership within a map class. Thus, a separate field key to map classes would be redundant and would provide less information than a vegetation key. Vegetation (floristic and physiognomic) criteria should predominate in the key. Environmental factors may be used sparingly (see Subsection 5.2.3). If the vegetation classification is well documented and appropriately scaled, there should be limited need for evaluating environmental criteria.

Field keys are intended to be applied within an observed area of vegetation that is relatively internally homogeneous and that contains a sufficiently adequate amount of the floristic elements of the type to which the classification would assign it for accurate diagnosis. Typically, this area is defined as either a stand or, at least, an adequately large and representative portion of a stand (e.g., a releve). Where possible, it can be helpful for the key to specify the estimated minimum size of the observation area over which it is intended to be applied.

It is recommended that field key users compare the vegetation type that was arrived at by following the key with the [more comprehensive] description of the type. If the observed vegetation seems a poor fit with the description, then the observer should attempt the key process again, paying attention to possible alternative paths through the key to the path followed on the first attempt.

Field keys are the primary means of diagnosis of vegetation types in the field for the purpose of map validation, which evaluates project performance for overall thematic accuracy (see http://science.nature.nps.gov/im/inventory/veg/guidance.cfm). Field keys also are the primary means of diagnosis of vegetation types for the class-by-class thematic accuracy assessment of vegetation maps (Lea and Curtis 2010). In these applications, the field diagnosis using the key is assumed to be the highest source of accuracy possible (at 100%, unless demonstrated otherwise). Therefore, careful attention to writing accurate and consistent diagnostic keys and testing them in the field is important in the NPS Vegetation Inventory.

Several rules of thumb may be employed in testing keys. Keys are often created (and should be created, whenever possible) from the floristic data in classified vegetation plots. They can be "back-tested" in the office, against these "training data" plots, as a means of quality control. Ideally, the result of keying the data from the plot would match the key diagnosis 100% of the time. If this is not the case, individual discrepancies should be assessed and corrected or justified (e.g., adjusting the key, reassigning individual plots, attributing occasional mismatches to sampling variability, etc.). In the field, the diagnosis that has been made by a key user in a previously unsampled ("test data") vegetation stand may be tested against an independent assessment by a subject-matter expert considered to be a higher source of accuracy (e.g., the ecologist creating the classification). If the results should match at least 80-90% of the time (depending on the thematic resolution of the classification), this suggests that more work on the key may be needed.

5.2 Characteristics of Field Keys
5.2.1 Dichotomous versus Multichotomous Keys
Field keys may be dichotomous (requiring multiple steps, but restricted to a two condition choice (a couplet) at each step or multichotomous (requiring fewer steps, but with some steps having three or more conditions at individual steps). The advantage of a dichotomous key is that the user may focus carefully on only two sets of possible conditions at each step. The advantage of a multichotomous key is that there are fewer steps to consider, at each point of which a decision error might be made. The desirable quality of comprehensiveness in a key (see below) requires that each combination of pairwise diagnostic comparisons be mutually exclusive of one another. Multichotomies increase the number of pairwise comparisons in a factorial manner (one comparison for a dichotomy (or couplet), three comparisons for a trichotomy, six comparisons for a four-parted step, etc.). They rapidly become more complex with more conditions. Because of the proliferation of pairwise differentiations involved, multichotomous keys are often necessarily nodal (see Subsection 5.2.2) and, thus, require more expertise and subjectivity.

In general, dichotomous keys are preferable for non-expert use. Multichotomous keys are acceptable if the number of conditions required of the user to evaluate at each step is limited. The choice of whether to incorporate multichotomous steps or not may depend on the nature of relationships between vegetation types classified, diagnostic criteria selected, and the quality and completeness of the data used to build the key.

5.2.2 Comprehensive versus Nodal Keys
In a comprehensive key, all possible field conditions are accounted for, and the user is forced to a fairly objective choice at each decision point (couplet). In a nodal key, the user is required to select the best choice from several that are offered at a decision point that reflect non-overlapping conditions. This requires more subjectivity and expertise. While both types of keys are diagnostic in that they simplify a multivariate phenomenon into a determination based on a

relative few of its many characteristics, the nodal key is more oriented toward the nodum (central or typical expression) of the type concept, whereas the comprehensive key seeks to minimize the amount of conceptual overlap between types and the amount of user discretion in the diagnosis and emphasizes more precise conceptual boundaries between types. In Figure 2 (Chapter 2), a nodal key might fail to give an unambiguous answer for vegetation stands that are represented by the shaded sections of the gradient. A comprehensive key might give a more definitive answer in these stands (i.e., greater chances of both a correct answer and a wrong answer). (For a discussion of sources of higher accuracy in correctness of reference data, see Lea and Curtis (2010), section 3.1).

Ideally, diagnostic field keys are comprehensive because the purpose of a key is to force a clear distinction between types. A comprehensive key will cover all known vegetation types in the study (park) area in a mutually exclusive (non-overlapping) and complete manner. Comprehensive keys address uncertainties ("ecotones") between intergrading vegetation types by rigidly defining discrete boundaries between types, even though limits of field observation may require these predicted diagnostic boundaries to be somewhat imprecise. The advantages of a comprehensive key are (1) since every stand can be placed somewhere within the classification scheme objectively, use of the key requires less *a priori* experience with the classification, and (2) the key is more objective (answers between observers will tend to be more consistent, even if wrong). Disadvantages include (1) the accuracy of the key depends more on the quality of the data used to build it, and (2) the key does not allow for as much individual interpretation (including by an expert).

Nodal keys are more restricted to describing the more "typical" expressions of classified types. They address differences between types by allowing the user some latitude in determining the best fit in the classification for an individual stand. The disadvantages of a nodal key are: (1) ambiguous stands (ecotones) must be addressed subjectively, (2) more *a priori* experience with the classification is required of the user, and (3) conditions in the key tend to be more subjective in assessment and, therefore, may lead to inconsistencies even between expert observers, especially for confusing or intergrading stands. Advantages include: (1) the accuracy of the key depends less on the quality of the data used to build it, and (2) expert judgment (which may be more accurate) can more easily overrule diagnostics. Nodal keys may be more useful when the quantity and quality of quantitative stand (plot) data that can narrow the range of diagnostic conditions are less available to the key writer. Multichotomous keys tend to be nodal because the factorial proliferation of all possible pairwise differences at each multichotomous decision point makes it difficult to account for all possible conditions in one of the answers.

The following dichotomy (couplet) (from Young et al. 2009) is comprehensive in that an intermediate condition between the conditions 5a and 5b cannot exist.

5a Conifers contributing at least 25% cover to the tree layers (overstory and understory) ..go to 6
5b Conifers absent or contributing less than 25% cover to the tree layers .... go to 24

The following two dichotomies (couplets) (from Lea et al. in prep.) are also comprehensive in that an intermediate condition between the conditions 6a and 6b cannot exist (although alternate individual criteria can determine either condition). When using field keys, the user should pay strict attention to logical operators such as "and" and "or."

6a Boxelder (*Acer negundo*) has greater than or equal to 40% relative cover (among all trees) and greater than or equal to 40% absolute cover)…………….……………*Acer negundo* **Forest**

6b Either the relative (among all trees) or absolute cover of boxelder (*Acer negundo*), or both, is less than 40% ……………………………………………………………………………………………go to 7

12a The combined absolute cover of both sweet gum (*Liquidambar styraciflua*) and chinquapin oak (*Quercus muehlenbergii*) is greater than the combined absolute cover of both water oak (*Quercus nigra*) and cherrybark oak (*Quercus pagoda*)………………...………………………………… ……………………………………*Liquidambar styraciflua - Carya illinoinensis - Quercus nigra* **Forest**

12b The combined absolute cover of both sweet gum (*Liquidambar styraciflua*) and chinquapin oak (*Quercus muehlenbergii*) is less than or equal to the combined absolute cover of both water oak (*Quercus nigra*) and cherrybark oak (*Quercus pagoda*)……………………………………… ……………………………………………………………*Quercus pagoda - Quercus nigra* **Forest**

The following dichotomy (couplet) (from Young et al. 2009) is nodal in that an intermediate condition between the conditions 14a and 14b may exist (e.g., a mid-slope setting that is partly exposed, with a community that is only somewhat oak and pine-dominated). It also has two distinct criteria (one related to canopy composition and dominance and the other related to topographic position) that could conflict (e.g., a forest with a mixed dominance, mesophytic canopy might occur in a more exposed topography than stream bottoms, coves, ravines, or concave slopes).

14a Mesophytic forests, often with mixed canopy dominance, of stream bottoms, coves, ravines, and concave slopes ……………………………………………………………………………………15
14b Drier, oak- and/or pine-dominated forests and woodlands of various, usually more exposed topography ……………………………………………………………………………………………17

The following five-part multichotomy (quintuplet) (adapted from Keeler-Wolf et al. 2005) is also nodal. While it describes more typical stands of each type well, it is less precise as to thresholds between the types (e.g., if *Quercus cornelius-mulleri*, *Yucca schidigera*, and *Coleogyne ramosissima* are all prominent in a stand, it may be ambiguous as to whether to select condition T.I.B.1 or condition T.I.B.2).

T.I.B.1. *Juniperus californica* is the characteristic short tree or tall shrub, mixing with the scrub oak *Quercus cornelius-mulleri*. The small shrub *Coleogyne ramosissima* is characteristic in the understory…………………………………………………………………………………… *Juniperus californica - Quercus cornelius-mulleri / Coleogyne ramosissima* **Woodland Association**

T.I.B.2. *Juniperus californica* occurs as a tall shrub or low tree with the shrubby *Yucca schidigera*, and the short shrub *Coleogyne ramosissima* characteristic in the understory. *Juniperus californica / Coleogyne ramosissima - Yucca schidigera* **Woodland Association**

T.I.B.3. *Juniperus californica* occurs with *Yucca schidigera.* *Coleogyne ramosissima* is absent or present at very low cover, and the medium tall bunch grass *Pleuraphis rigida* is characteristic of the understory
***Juniperus californica - (Yucca schidigera) / Pleuraphis rigida* Woodland Association**

T.I.B.4. *Juniperus californica* is the principal tall shrub or small tree over a relatively simple understory characterized by the low shrub *Coleogyne ramosissima.*
***Juniperus californica / Coleogyne ramosissima* Woodland Association**

T.I.B.5. *Juniperus californica* is the characteristic small tree or large shrub with a mixture of other shrub species including the characteristic yucca-like *Nolina parryi.*
Juniperus californica / Nolina parryi Woodland Association

Errors produced by using a comprehensive key reflect limitations in the products, including the key itself and are more repeatable test of error rates between different users. Errors produced by nodal keys tend to be influenced more by limitations in user knowledge.

In most cases for the NPS Vegetation Inventory, including the use of the key for thematic accuracy assessment of a vegetation map, comprehensiveness in a field key is a desirable attribute, whenever possible. Within the NPS Vegetation Inventory, described types usually are well supported by multiple plots with quantitative stand data. Moreover, field key users are often not experts in vegetation ecology. Nodal aspects to a field key are acceptable and may be necessary, especially in cases in which quantitative observational data on vegetation types are very limited and it would be risky to attempt to define precise diagnostic thresholds.

The above examples are presented as illustrative examples from field keys from NPS vegetation inventory projects, to show different balances of comprehensive versus nodal attributes. Full versions of these keys are presented in Appendix D (Exhibits 4, 5, and 6).

5.2.3 Considerations for and Pitfalls in Writing Field Keys
Because the classification itself is built upon floristic criteria, the field key criteria ideally should be able to diagnose vegetation types without incorporating environmental, geographic, or other non-floristic criteria. That is, if two types can be diagnosed only by environmental or geographic criteria, then they are arguably the same type or, at least, cannot be adequately described as distinct with the vegetation data at hand. Additionally, many field users will possess reliable plant species identification and cover estimation skills, but cannot be expected to always identify conditions that require experience in other disciplines (e.g., identifying difficult wetland or hydrologic conditions or soil or geologic substrates).

Nevertheless, incorporating some easily identified and/or well-explained environmental or geographic conditions can enhance the accuracy of a field key when floristic data that enable a more accurate diagnosis are limited. Appropriate environmental criteria should be conditions that are easily recognized by a layperson (e.g., (1) the vegetation is situated on a slope greater than 10 per cent versus on more level ground, (2) the vegetation is above 3,000 feet in elevation versus at or below 3,000 feet, (3) the cover of exposed rock in the observed area is greater than 3% versus less than or equal to 3%, (4) the vegetation is located in ecoregion A versus in ecoregion B (with the location of the ecoregion boundaries given). For projects that cross multiple ecoregions that have analogous, but distinct, vegetation types in each ecoregion (e.g., the National Capital Region parks, the Appalachian Trail), the practice of restricting types by ecoregion as partial or complete field key criteria may be more accurate than diagnosing types whose descriptions have been derived from a limited number of observations. If ecoregional influence is rather strong, or there are other large environmental gradients that can be evaluated precisely (e.g., elevation), it may be preferable to write separate keys (or "sub-keys) to each ecoregion (or elevation class). This will require some redundant treatment between the "sub-keys" for types that cross ecoregion (or elevation class) boundaries.

Environmental conditions that may require specialized skills or experience beyond identifying flora or estimating cover should be avoided or minimized in a key. Examples include terms such as "anthropogenic" disturbance, wetlands, and specific geologic substrates or soil types. Moreover, simpler terms that are more easily understood but which may be interpreted inconsistently by different observers as to meaning or degree (e.g., "swale," "floodplain," or "catastrophic" disturbance) also should be avoided or minimized.

Specificity is important in a field key in order to minimize key errors due to subjectivity between observers, including different experts. This is an important consideration for assessing mapping project performance, as in map validation or in assessing the map for reliability to the user, as in accuracy assessment (Lea and Curtis 2010). Subjective terms that define vegetation abundance such as "dominant" or "co-dominant," should be defined quantitatively (dominance or co-dominance can usually be defined as a per cent of relative cover comprised by an individual species or "ecological superspecies" (= group of ecologically related species that have equivalent diagnostic value for purposes of a key condition). In most cases, it may be preferable to state a quantitative threshold of either absolute or relative cover for a species at each couplet, since the degree of dominance by a species will vary by type, as the plot data usually will suggest.

As discussed in Chapter 2, it is somewhat uncommon that a single species abundance threshold reliably diagnoses a type. Even where this is the case, it is rare that the number of plots observed for the type will be sufficient to define an abundance threshold for the species very precisely. Often, an accurate diagnosis will rely upon the co-occurrence of or the combined cover of two or more ecologically similar species (ecological "superspecies"). This is because two or more species with similar habitat preferences often occur as [more or less] ecological vicariants of one another within a vegetation type. On the observation scale of a single plot, these vicariants will tend to compete with and exclude one another, so that the particular abundance of one vicariant as compared to another vicariant is relatively insignificant at these small observation scales. As a general rule, the number of a pool of vicariant diagnostic species will increase when diagnoses of floristically broader vegetation groups (e.g., between higher levels of a formal hierarchical classification or between *ad hoc* or artificial groups that are separated in the early steps of a diagnostic field key) are being made.

If it is necessary to generalize as to a suite of plant species that are characteristic of certain environmental conditions, then the key should name the plant species that are characteristic of those conditions. For example, if the key user is asked to evaluate whether a stand is dominated by "wetland" or "mesophytic" species or species of calcareous sites, then a list of applicable species for the area should be provided (see Appendix D, Exhibit 5).

Although field keys may progress downward through levels of a vegetation classification hierarchy (e.g., a natural key), there is no need for a key to strictly adhere to this approach. Often, classified types that are fairly unrelated in a formal hierarchy may intergrade closely on the ground and the most accurate differentiations and diagnoses may require an artificial key. These include the examples in Subsection 2.3.3, in which a type assigned to one USNVC class (Forest and Woodland, or Mesomorphic Tree Vegetation) may subtly intergrade with a type from a different USNVC class (Shrubland and Grassland, or Mesomorphic Shrub and Herb Vegetation) Class), based on cover differences in a single tree species. Differentiation between the two relatively unrelated types may need to occur in late, as well as in early, couplets in the field key (i.e., an artificial key approach).

If a field key to [thematically] low level classes (e.g., USNVC associations) in a hierarchy is constructed, the most accurate possible field key to higher levels of the hierarchy (e.g., USNVC groups) likely would be constructed by first substituting the higher level type names for the lower level type names in the key, then by eliminating all couplets that lead to the same high level type name (e.g., the same USNVC Group) and, finally, by inserting that high level type name as the answer to the parent condition of the eliminated couplets. This helps to increase key accuracy by ensuring that individual differentiations between unrelated low level types are retained, rather than lost by focus on the more generalized differences that are usually made between the higher level types.

Species that are apparent to the observer for short periods or sporadically during the seasons for which the key is to be used (e.g., winter annuals in semi-desert areas, spring ephemerals in deciduous forests) should be avoided. If such species make good diagnostics such that their inclusion is desirable for the times when they are apparent, then the key should incorporate redundant conditions that allow the user to also key to the correct type when their apparent absence may be due to phenology or other seasonal conditions, rather than to true absence.

Redundancy (i.e., more than one way to arrive at a correct answer) makes a field key more accurate. Species that are absolutely diagnostic (high fidelity and high constancy) of a type are very rare. Usually, species that have high fidelity to a type (i.e. ecologically sensitive species) do not have high constancy in that type, whereas highly constant species tend to be successful species that also are constant and/or abundant in other types (i.e., have low fidelity to a type).

5.3 Sources of Diagnostic Information for Field Keys
5.3.1 Classification Plots
Classification plots are the primary source of information for creating diagnostic field keys of vegetation types on a local scale. Once vegetation classes have been defined, differential species between progressively finer groups can be derived from species by plots tables of classified types or from formal methods such as discriminant analysis (McCune and Grace 2002) or indicator species analysis (Dufrêne and Legendre 1997, McCune and Grace 2002). The classification methods themselves can assist with the construction of field key hierarchies by identifying progressively more differentiating gaps in the data set. For example, the most logical early dichotomies in the field key often correspond to early partitions in a cluster analysis dendrogram or to larger gaps between groups of observations along low order axes of an ordination diagram.

5.3.2 Observation Plots

When quantitative data from plots are limited, additional local field observations of stands, perhaps made during map verification (Figure 1) may help establish appropriate diagnostic thresholds between groups. It is helpful if a plot-based classification has been completed prior to these observations, so that the nodal tendencies of types are known and the range of possible diagnostic threshold conditions be narrowed. At that point, transitional stands that show conditions within those ranges can be observed, and the diagnostic thresholds can be refined to be more precise.

5.3.3 Other Sources

When diagnostic criteria between two or more types from field observations are not precise, mapping criteria may be used to further refine the diagnostics. From a remote sensing perspective, mappers see more stands than field ecologists can observe or that can be sampled by plots and they can often more readily estimate cover at stand scales. Subsection 2.3.3 of Chapter 2 describes how this approach can be employed.

6.0 Reporting Requirements

When the vegetation descriptions and field keys are completed, the classification ecologist submits the vegetation classification report section to the mapping investigator, the NPS oversight team, and others for review. If a separate team has completed the classification plot field sampling, it may be appropriate to have that team write parts of the methods section. Peer review of the descriptions and project methods is encouraged.

The vegetation classification section(s) of a NPS Vegetation Inventory report should include:

(1) A description of the methods used to create the vegetation types, including:

- Relevant background information (about the site, etc.)

- Sampling design. If the team that is tasked with field data collection has written these methods (as appropriate) they will be incorporated into the classification report.

- Field plot sampling methods. If the team that is tasked with field data collection has written these methods (as appropriate) they will be incorporated into the classification report.

- Quantitative and/or qualitative analysis methods

- Results of analysis, including a list of the vegetation types

(2) For each vegetation type recognized, a local description, including:

- The placement of each vegetation type within the current content of the U.S. National Vegetation Classification (USNVC) (where possible). This requirement may be incorporated into the list and/or local descriptions

- The relationship of each vegetation type to each map class used in the project. This requirement may be incorporated into the list and/or local descriptions

(3) A field key to the vegetation types of the park

Local descriptions and field keys may be included as appendices to the classification report.

Additionally, the classification ecologist should annotate, in the PLOTS database, all classification plots that have been collected by the project, to the classified type, wherever possible. Most data collected for PLOTS will have been entered by the field data collection team.

When the final drafts of the classification report and PLOTS database are completed and sensitive data issues (if any) are resolved, these are posted on the NPS Vegetation Inventory web site and may be posted at other public web sites, such as VegBank (Ecological Society of America 2008). It is intended that public access to PLOTS data will allow NPS plot data to be merged with state, regional, and/or national data in order to further the public purpose of the development of the USNVC and to available for other national management or research needs.

Literature Cited

Anderson, M., P. Bourgeron, M. T. Bryer, R. Crawford, L. Engelking, D. Faber-Langendoen, M. Gallyoun, K. Goodin, D. H. Grossman, S. Landaal, K. Metzler, K. D. Patterson, M. Pyne, M. Reid, L. Sneddon, and A. S. Weakley. 1998. International classification of ecological communities: Terrestrial vegetation of the United States. Volume II. The National Vegetation Classification System: list of types. The Nature Conservancy, Arlington, VA, USA.

Berendsohn, W.G. 1995. The concept of "potential taxa" in databases. Taxon 44:207-212.

Box, E. O. 1981. Macroclimate and plant forms: An introduction to predictive modeling in phytogeography. Dr. W. Junk, The Hague, The Netherlands.

Brewer, C., B. Schwind, R. Warbington, W. Clerke, P. Krosse, L. Suring, and M. Schanta. 2005. Section 3: Existing Vegetation Mapping Protocol. In: Brohman, R. and L. Bryant, eds. Existing vegetation classification and mapping technical guide. General Technical Report WO-67. U. S. Department of Agriculture, Forest Service, Ecosystem Management Coordination Staff, Washington, DC, USA.

Brohman, R. and L. Bryant, eds. 2005. Existing vegetation classification and mapping technical guide. General Technical Report WO-67. U.S. Department of Agriculture, Forest Service, Ecosystem Management Coordination Staff, Washington, DC, USA.

Bruelheide, H. 2000. A new measure of fidelity and its application to defining species groups. Journal of Vegetation Science 11:167-178.

Comer, P., D. Faber-Langendoen, R. Evans, S. Gawler, C. Josse, G. Kittel, S. Menard, M. Pyne, M. Reid, K. Schulz, K. Snow, and J. Teague. 2003. Ecological Systems of the United States: A working classification of U.S. terrestrial systems. NatureServe, Arlington, VA, USA.

Condit, R., R. Perez, and N. Daguerre. 2011. Trees of Panama and Costa Rica. Princeton University Press, Princeton, NJ, USA.

Cowardin, L.M., V. Carter, F.C. Golet, and E.T. LaRoe. 1979. Classification of wetlands and deepwater habitats of the United States. FWS/OBS-79/31. U.S. Department of Interior, Fish and Wildlife Service, Washington, DC, USA.

Curtis, J.T. 1959. The vegetation of Wisconsin: An ordination of plant communities. University of Wisconsin Press, Madison, WI, USA.

Czaplewski, R. L. 2003. Accuracy assessment of maps of forest condition: statistical design and methodological considerations. Pages 115 to 140 in Wulder, M. A. and S. E. Franklin, editors. Remote Sensing of Forest Environments: Concepts and Case Studies. Kluwer Academic Publishers, Boston, MA, USA.

Daubenmire, R.F. 1968. Plant communities: A textbook of plant synecology. New York: Harper and Row.

Di Gregorio, Antonio; Jansen, Louisa J.M. 1996. FAO land cover classification: A dichotomous, modular-hierarchical approach. Rome, Italy: Food and Agriculture Organization of the United Nations.

Driscoll, R. S., D. L. Merkel, D. L. Radloff, D. E. Snyder, and J. S. Hagihara. 1984. An ecological land classification framework for the United States. Department of Agriculture, U.S. Forest Service Miscellaneous Publication 1439. U.S. Department of Agriculture Forest Service, Washington, DC, USA.

Dufrêne, M. and P. Legendre. 1997. Species assemblages and indicator species: the need for a flexible asymmetrical approach. Ecological Monographs 67:345-366.

Ecological Society of America, Vegetation Classification Panel. 2008. VegBank. Online database. [Available: http://vegbank.org].

Faber-Langendoen, D., J. Drake, S. Gawler, G. Kittel, S. Menard, C. Nordman, M. Pyne, M. Reid, L. Sneddon, K. Schulz, J. Teague, M. Russo, K. Snow, and P. Comer. 2010. Macrogroups and groups for the revised U.S. National Vegetation Classification. + appendices. NatureServe, Arlington, VA, USA.

Faber-Langendoen, D., D. L. Tart, and R. H. Crawford. 2009. Contours of the revised U.S. National Vegetation Standard. Bulletin of the Ecological Society of America 90:87–93.

Faber-Langendoen, D., D. Tart, A. Gray, B. Hoagland, O. Huber, C. Josse, S. Karl, T. Keeler-Wolf, D. Meidinger, S. Ponomarenko, J-P. Saucier, A. Velázquez-Montes, and A. Weakley. 2008 (In prep). Guidelines for an integrated physiognomic–floristic approach to vegetation classification. Hierarchy Revisions Working Group, U. S. Geological Survey, Federal Geographic Data Committee, Vegetation Subcommittee, Reston, VA, USA.

Federal Geographic Data Committee. 1997. Vegetation Subcommittee. Vegetation Classification Standard. FGDC-STD-005. U. S. Geological Survey, Federal Geographic Data Committee, Vegetation Subcommittee, Reston, VA. USA. [Available: http://www.fgdc.gov/standards/documents/standards/vegetation/vegclass.pdf].

Federal Geographic Data Committee. 2008. Vegetation Subcommittee. National Vegetation Classification Standard, version 2. FGDC-STD-005-2008. Reston, VA: Federal Geographic Data Committee, U.S. Geological Survey. [Available: http://www.fgdc.gov/standards/documents/standards/vegetation/vegclass.pdf]

Fleming, G. P. 2007. Ecological communities of the Potomac Gorge in Virginia: composition, floristics, and environmental dynamics. Natural Heritage Technical Report 07-12. Virginia Department of Conservation and Recreation, Division of Natural Heritage. Richmond, VA, USA. + appendices.

Fosberg, F.R. 1961. A classification of vegetation for general purposes. Tropical Ecology 2:1–28.

Franklin, J.F. and C.T. Dyrness. 1973. Natural vegetation of Washington and Oregon. USDA Forest Service General Technical Report PNW-8. Pacific Northwest Forest and Range Experiment Station. Portland, OR, USA.

Gabriel, H.W. and S.S. Talbot. 1984. Glossary of landscape and vegetation ecology for Alaska. Alaska Technical Report 10. U.S. Department of the Interior, Bureau of Land Management, Washington, DC, USA.

Gauch, H.G., Jr. 1982. Multivariate analysis in community ecology. Cambridge University Press. Cambridge, England.

Gauch, H.G., Jr. and R.H. Whittaker. 1981. Hierarchical classification of community data. Journal of Ecology 69:537-557.

Gerwing, J.J. 2004. Life history diversity among six species of canopy lianas in an old-growth forest of the eastern Brazilian Amazon. Forest Ecology and Management 190:57-72.

Gleason, H.A. 1917. The structure and development of the plant association. Bulletin of the Torrey Botanical Club 44:463–481.

Gleason, H.A. 1926. The individualistic concept of the plant association. Bulletin of the Torrey Botanical Club 53:7–26.

Grossman, D. H., D. Faber-Langendoen, A. S. Weakley, M. Anderson, P. Bourgeron, R. Crawford, K. Goodin, S. Landaal, K. Metzler, K. Patterson, M. Pyne, M. Reid, and L. Sneddon. 1998. International classification of ecological communities: Terrestrial vegetation of the United States. Volume I: The National Vegetation Classification System: Development, status, and applications. The Nature Conservancy, Arlington, VA, USA.

Helms, J. 1998. The dictionary of forestry. Society of American Foresters, Bethesda, MD, USA.

Hill, M.O. 1979. TWINSPAN - a FORTRAN program for arranging multivariate data in an ordered two-way table by classification of the individuals and attributes. Ecology and Systematics, Cornell University, Ithaca, NY, USA.

Hill, M.O. and H.G. Gauch. 1980. Detrended correspondence analysis: an improved ordination technique. Vegetatio 42:47–58.

Jennings, Michael D., D. Faber-Langendoen, O. L. Loucks, R. K. Peet, and D. Roberts. 2009. Standards for associations and alliances of the U.S. National Vegetation Classification. Ecological Monographs 79:173–199. + appendices. [Available: http://www.esa.org/vegweb/docFiles/ESA_Guidelines_Version_5.2.pdf; http://esapubs.org/archive/mono/M079/006/default.htm].

Keeler-Wolf, T., S. San, and D. Hickson. 2005. Vegetation classification of Joshua Tree National Park, Riverside and San Bernardino Counties, California. Report submitted to the National Park Service. California Department of Fish and Game Wildlife and Habitat Data Analysis Branch. Sacramento, CA, USA.

Kent, M. and P. Coker. 1992. Vegetation description and analysis. Belhaven Press, London, England.

Kimmins, J.P. 1997. Forest ecology: a foundation for sustainable management. Second edition. Prentice Hall, Upper Saddle River, NJ, USA.

Kruskal, J.B. 1964. Nonmetric multidimensional scaling: a numerical method. Psychometrika 29:115-129.

Kuchler, A.W. 1969. Natural and cultural vegetation. The Professional Geographer 21:383-385.

Kuchler, A.W. and I.S. Zonneveld. 1988. Vegetation mapping. Kluwer Academic Publishers. Boston, MA, USA.

Lambert, J.M. and W.T. Williams. 1962. Multivariate methods in plant ecology IV: nodal analysis. Journal of Ecology 50:775-802.

Lea, C. 2000. Plant communities of the Potomac Gorge and their relationship to fluvial factors. M, S, thesis. George Mason University. Fairfax, VA, USA.

Lea, C. 2008. A report card for the National Vegetation Classification: Is it a standard in practice? Presentation at Organized Oral Session OOS-19. Approaches for linking vegetation classification, vegetation mapping, and remote sensing technologies. Ecological Society of America Annual Meeting. Milwaukee, WI, USA. August 7, 2008.

Lea, C. 2009. New approaches to applying the National Vegetation Classification. Poster presentation at Biennial Conference of the George Wright Society. Portland, OR, USA. March 2-6, 2009.

Lea, C. and A. C. Curtis. 2010. Thematic accuracy assessment procedures: National Park Service Vegetation Inventory, Version 2.0. Natural Resource Report NPS/2010/NRR—2010/204. U. S. Department of the Interior, National Park Service, Fort Collins, CO, USA. [Available: http://science.nature.nps.gov/im/inventory/veg/guidance.cfm].

Lea, C. et al. 2011. Field methods for vegetation classification: National Park Service Vegetation Inventory, Version 2.0. Natural Resource Report. U. S. Department of the Interior, National Park Service, Fort Collins, CO, USA. [Available: http://science.nature.nps.gov/im/inventory/veg/guidance.cfm].

Lea, C., R. Waltermire, and C. Nordman. In prep. Vegetation classification and mapping, Vicksburg National Military Park, Mississippi. Natural Resource Technical Report. U. S. Department of the Interior, National Park Service, Lafayette, LA, USA.

Lincoln, R, G. Boxshall, and P. Clark. 1998. A dictionary of ecology, evolution and systematics. Cambridge University Press, New York, NY, USA.

McCune, B. and J.B. Grace. 2002. Analysis of ecological communities. MjM Software Design, Gleneden Beach, OR, USA.

McCune, B. and M.J. Mefford. 1999. PC-ORD. Multivariate analysis of ecological data, version 4.0. [software application]. MjM Software Design, Gleneden Beach, OR, USA.

Moses, C.S., A. Nayegandhi, J. Brock, and R. Beavers. 2010. USGS-NPS Servicewide benthic mapping program (SBMP) workshop report. U.S. Geological Survey Open-File Report 2010-1194. U.S. Department of the Interior. U. S. Geological Survey, Reston, VA, USA.

Mueller-Dombois, D. and H. Ellenberg. 1974. Aims and Methods of Vegetation Ecology. John Wiley and Sons, New York, NY, USA.

National Park Service. 1992. NPS-75: Natural resources inventory and monitoring guideline. U.S. Department of Interior, National Park Service. Washington, DC, USA.

NatureServe. 2009. NatureServe Explorer: An online encyclopedia of life [web application]. Version 7.1. NatureServe, Arlington, VA, USA. [Available: http://www.natureserve.org/explorer].

Office of Management and Budget. 1990. Circular A-16: Coordination of geographic information and related spatial data activities. Office of Management and Budget. Washington, DC, USA.

Office of Management and Budget. 2002. Circular A-16: Coordination of geographic information and related spatial data activities. Office of Management and Budget. Washington, DC, USA. [Available: http://www.whitehouse.gov/omb/circulars/a016/a016_rev.html].

Peet R.K. 2008. A decade of effort by the ESA Vegetation Panel leads to a new federal standard. Ecological Society of America Bulletin 89:210–211.

Peet, R.K., T.R. Wentworth and P.S. White. 1998. A flexible, multipurpose method for recording vegetation composition and structure. Castanea 63:262-274.

Pielou, E.C. 1984. The interpretation of ecological data: A primer of classification and ordination. John Wiley & Sons, New York, NY, USA.

Poore, M.E.D. 1956. The use of phytosociological methods in ecological investigations IV: general discussion of phytosociological methods. Journal of Ecology 44:28-50.

Pyle, R.L. 2004. Taxonomer: a relational data model for managing information relevant to taxonomic research. PhyloInformatics 1:1-54.

Rapp, J., D. Wang, D. Capen, E. Thompson, and T. Lautzenheiser. 2005. Evaluating error in using the National Vegetation Classification System for ecological community mapping in northern New England, USA. Natural Areas Journal 25:46–54.

Rice, P., W. Gustafson, E. W. Schweiger, D. Manier, D. Shorrock, C. Lea, and B. Frakes. In prep. Vegetation classification and mapping project report, Little Bighorn Battlefield

National Monument. Natural Resource Technical Report. U.S. Department of the Interior, National Park Service, Fort Collins, CO, USA.

Roberts, D.W. 1989. Fuzzy systems vegetation theory. Vegetatio 66:71–80.

Society for Range Management. 1989. A glossary of terms used in range management. Society for Range Management, Denver, CO, USA.

Tart, D., C. Williams, J. DiBenedetto, E. Crowe, M. Girard, H. Gordon, K. Sleavin, M. Manning, J. Haglund, B. Short, and D. Wheeler. 2005. Section 2: Existing vegetation classification protocol. Pages 2-1 to 2-34 in Brohman, R. and L. Bryant, editors. Existing vegetation classification and mapping technical guide. General Technical Report WO-67. U.S. Department of Agriculture Forest Service, Ecosystem Management Coordination Staff, Washington, DC, USA.

ter Braak, C.J.F. 1990. CANOCO — a FORTRAN program for canonical community ordination by [detrended] [canonical] correspondence analysis, principal components analysis and redundancy analysis, version 3.10. Microcomputer Power, Ithaca, New York, USA.

ter Braak, C.J.F. (ed.) 1996. Unimodal models to relate species to environment. DLO-Agricultural Mathematics Group, Wageningen, The Netherlands.

The Nature Conservancy and Environmental Systems Research Institute. 1994. Standardized National Vegetation Classification System: NBS/NPS Vegetation Mapping Program. Report prepared for the National Biological Survey and National Park Service. The Nature Conservancy, Arlington, VA and Redlands, CA, USA.

Tichy, L. 2002. JUICE, software for vegetation classification. Journal of Vegetation Science 13:451–453.

Tichy, L. and J. Holt. 2006. JUICE, Program for management, analysis, and classification of ecological data. Program manual. Vegetation Science Group. Masaryk University BRNO, Czech Republic. [Available: http://www.sci.muni.cz/botany/juice/JUICEman_all.pdf].

United Nations Educational, Scientific, and Cultural Organization. 1973. International classification and mapping of vegetation. Series 6. Ecology and conservation, Paris, France.

Vanderhorst, J. P., J. Jeuck, and S. C. Gawler. 2007. Vegetation classification and mapping of New River Gorge National River, West Virginia. Technical Report NPS/NER/NRTR— 2007/092. U. S. Department of the Interior, National Park Service. Philadelphia, PA, USA.

Westhoff, V. and E. Van der Maarel. 1978. The Braun-Blanquet approach. In: R.H. Whittaker (editor) Classification of plant communities. Dr. W. Junk Publishers, The Hague, The Netherlands.

Whittaker, R.H. 1956. Vegetation of the Great Smoky Mountains. Ecological Monographs 22:1–44.

Whittaker, R.H. 1962. Classification of natural communities. Botanical Review 28:1–239.

Whittaker, R.H. 1973. Approaches to classifying vegetation. Pp. 323-354 in R.H. Whitaker, (editor). Ordination and Classification of Communities. Handbook of Vegetation Science 5. Dr. W. Junk Publishers, The Hague, The Netherlands.

Whittaker, R.H. 1975. Evolution of species diversity in land communities. Evolutionary Biology 10:1–67.

Wilson, M.V., and A. Shmida. 1984. Measuring beta diversity with presence-absence data. Journal of Ecology 72:1055-1064.

Young, J., G. Fleming, W. Cass, and C. Lea. 2009. Vegetation of Shenandoah National Park in relation to environmental gradients, Version 2.0. Report to the National Park Service. U.S. Geological Survey, Virginia Natural Heritage Program, and U. S. Department of the Interior, National Park Service. Leetown, VA, USA.

Appendix A: The U.S. National Vegetation Classification and the National Vegetation Classification Standard

A.1 Current Role of the National Park Service in the Development of the U.S. National Vegetation Classification (USNVC)

The first version of this guidance (The Nature Conservancy and Environmental Systems Research Institute 1994) specified that NPS Vegetation Inventory use a consistent classification system and mapping protocol for vegetation types across all National Park System lands. This revised version modifies and clarifies that specification to require only that ecological classifications developed from local data be capable of being cross walked, as best as can be done, to the United States National Vegetation Classification (USNVC). This revised version encourages parks to use the USNVC directly for local classification schemes where possible and practical.

Because of increased federal involvement in the development of the USNVC since 1990, these NPS partnership activities reflect a broader inter-organizational commitment to a content development process on a national and even global scale. At the same time, because of a reduction in funds for implementing local NPS (park) inventory needs, the NPS Vegetation Inventory has eliminated contributing to development of the USNVC as a major objective of NPS projects. Instead, the NPS objective for classification activities within the NPS is to classify and describe vegetation at the local (park) level and to cross walk these classified units to the USNVC. Notwithstanding this shift in emphasis, local NPS projects that are funded by the Vegetation Inventory are expected to make plot data and other classification information available to the public, in conformance with federal policy (Office of Management and Budget 1990, 2002).

The NPS continues to support the direct development of the USNVC through its active participation on the FGDC Vegetation Subcommittee and the ESA Vegetation Panel and through occasional national funding initiatives with partners. USNVC development is an indirect objective of individual park projects primarily through their collecting local plot data in compliance with FGDC standards and making the data publicly available (FGDC 2008, Jennings et al. 2009).

A.2 History of the National Vegetation Classification Standard, 1990-2008

Development of a National Vegetation Classification Standard (NVCS), a protocol for the hierarchical taxonomy for vegetation, has been underway in the United States for several decades through work championed by The Nature Conservancy (TNC). NatureServe, then part of TNC, published its version of the standard, titled National Vegetation Classification System, in 1994 (The Nature Conservancy and Environmental Research Systems Institute 1994). This taxonomic hierarchy, which specified an uppermost system level, four intermediate physiognomic taxonomic levels, and two lower floristic taxonomic levels, was derived from previous work by the United Nations Educational, Scientific and Cultural Organization (1973) and by Driscoll et al. (1984).

In 1990 the U.S. Office of Management and Budget (OMB) revised Circular No. A-16 (Office of Management and Budget 1990) to further development of the Federal Geographic Data

Committee (FGDC). The purpose of the FGDC is to promote development of database systems, information standards and exchange formats, and guidelines to encourage data sharing and public access. In 1990, the FGDC established an interagency Vegetation Subcommittee with the Forest Service as chair and tasked this Subcommittee to develop standards for classifying and describing vegetation. By 1993, NPS was an active member of this subcommittee as well as being directly involved with TNC in developing and conducting an NPS Vegetation Mapping Program. Circular A-16 was revised again in 2002 by Executive Order 12906 (Office of Management and Budget 2002) to direct the FGDC to involve state, local, and tribal governments, academic institutions, professional societies, and the private sector in standards development. This change permitted the Vegetation Subcommittee to further develop ongoing relationships that it by then had established with both TNC and the Ecological Society of America (ESA). In addition to participating as a member of the Subcommittee, ESA, in conjunction with the FGDC, NatureServe, and other collaborators, formed a Panel on Vegetation Classification (Peet 2008). This Panel produced a document (Jennings et al. 2009) that provides guidance for a comprehensive vegetation classification in the United States and contributed significantly to the FGDC standard-revision process that was then underway.

In 1997, the Vegetation Subcommittee adopted as a federal standard (see Table 1) (Federal Geographic Data Committee 1997) a modified version of the TNC vegetation classification hierarchy for the NVCS. The FGDC version of the NVCS included the classification of planted and cultivated vegetation, in addition to the natural and semi-natural vegetation addressed by the TNC version. As a consequence, the FGDC version of the NVCS dropped the uppermost (system) level of the TNC hierarchy and increased the number of physiognomic levels from four to seven, partly to accommodate planted and cultivated vegetation. In other respects, the NVCS structure in the FGDC version remained largely as it was in the 1994 TNC version described by Grossman et al. (1998).

The FGDC 1997 standard specified content for vegetation types for each of the physiognomic levels as part of the standard itself. Because of the ongoing need for substantial data collection and analysis to define the content of the lowest two, floristic levels (i.e. specific nomenclature and definitions for Alliances and Associations), FGDC did not specify in the 1997 standard any content for these levels. Rather. comprehensive provisional content for these two floristic levels was developed regionally under the leadership of TNC and initially published for the United States (Anderson et al. 1998) as the U. S. National Vegetation Classification. Eventually, the TNC staff charged with maintenance of the USNVC provisional content became a part of a new organization, NatureServe. NatureServe currently maintains this provisional content in a digital database, with much of the information available publicly through a web application (NatureServe 2009).

It is important to distinguish between the National Vegetation Classification Standard (NVCS), which is a relatively static standard (i.e., a document) and the U.S. National Vegetation Classification (USNVC), which is the taxonomic content that is specified by that standard and is continually evolving (i.e., a database). The Federal Geographic Data Committee understood that vegetation taxonomy is an evolutionary process, that existing procedures and rules for establishing and revising FGDC standards would be too cumbersome to accommodate rapid taxonomic development and revision of thousands of individual vegetation types, and that the solution would be a dynamic content standard, rather than a static content standard.

A.3 Changes in the National Vegetation Classification Standard, 2008 and Beyond

Experience in use of the 1997 USNVCS led users to identify two major concerns: (1) applying the physiognomic levels of the hierarchy to ecological and resource management applications (Brohman and Bryant 2005; Faber-Langendoen et al. 2008) was difficult and (2) there was an immense need to update the standards for the floristic levels (Jennings et al. 2009). The FGDC Vegetation Subcommittee sponsored a working group (Faber-Langendoen et al. 2008) to address the first issue and drew largely upon the work of the ESA Panel (Jennings et al. 2009) to address the second issue. Using working group, Panel, and Subcommittee findings, the FGDC issued a revised NVCS in 2008 (Federal Geographic Data Committee 2008).

The 2008 revision presents a new hierarchy scheme (Faber-Langendoen et al. 2008, Federal Geographic Data Committee 2008) (see Table 1) of six new levels (three upper levels and three middle levels) that replace the seven physiognomic levels of the 1997 hierarchy (Federal Geographic Data Committee 1997; Grossman et al. 1998). The 2008 revision retains the two lower levels of the 1997 hierarchy (USNVCS Alliance and Association). Additionally, the 2008 revision specifies a separate taxonomic hierarchy for cultural vegetation (equivalent to planted/cultivated vegetation of the 1997 standard). In both hierarchies, the levels from top to bottom represent progressively finer thematic and ecological units. The criteria at each level apply to relatively natural, upland vegetation; the criteria may be applied somewhat differently for vegetation that is more strongly influenced by local factors, such as hydrology or anthropogenic disturbance. The three new mid-levels of the 2008 hierarchy fill the conceptual span between the 1997 Formation and the Alliance. (Adapted from Faber-Langendoen et al. 2008, 2010). Finally, while the content (vegetation types) for the upper (physiognomic) levels was presented as a static standard in the 1997 NVCS, the 2008 NVCS revision does not specify static content (types) for any level; rather it specifies standards for the proposal, acceptance, and tracking through time of content and provides as the current standard the most recently accepted versions of the types.

The 2008 NVCS framework uses considerably different classification criteria from that of the 1997 NVCS, partly in order to better conform to a "bottom up" approach that uses considerable existing floristic level knowledge at the Association level of the USNVC (see Table 1). The content (the units themselves) of the new upper and middle levels and the naming of the units themselves only recently have begun. It is expected that the upper and middle level units may serve as better and more ecologically meaningful vegetation map classes than did those of the 1997 NVCS. Since they are based more strongly on "bottom-up" criteria developed from considerable existing information at the USNVC Association level than were the former hierarchy units, it is expected that they will also provide map classes that relate more directly to lower hierarchy USNVC ecological classes. The USNVC revision also required a peer review process to establish definitive content (individual units) of all levels of the USNVC.

The 2008 NVCS framework uses considerably different classification criteria for the top six levels from those of the 1997 NVCS, partly in order to better conform to a "bottom up" approach that uses considerable existing floristic level knowledge at the Association level of the USNVC (see Table 1). Describing the content (the classification units themselves) of the new upper and middle levels and the naming of those units only recently have begun. It is expected that the upper and middle level units may serve as better and more ecologically meaningful vegetation map classes than did those of the 1997 NVCS. Since the new classification levels are based more

Table 1. Comparison of original and revised versions of the hierarchies of the National Vegetation Classification Standard (adapted from Faber-Langendoen et al. 2008, 2010).

1997 HIERARCHY			2008 HIERARCHY		
LEVEL		CRITERIA (GENERALIZED)	LEVEL		CRITERIA (GENERALIZED)
PHYSIOGNOMIC	Division	Vegetated vs. Non-vegetated	NONE		Vegetated vs. Non-vegetated
					Natural vs. Cultural
	Order	Dominant growth form			
	Class	Canopy cover of growth forms		Class	Growth form →← Moisture-Temperature
	Subclass	Leaf morphology / herb periodicity			
	Group	Leaf morphology / global climate		Subclass	Growth form →← Global climate
	Subgroup	Natural versus Cultural			
	Formation	Specific morphology of dominant growth forms / abiotic factors	UPPER	Formation	Growth form response to continental climate, topography, soils.
			MIDDLE	Division	Biogeographic species groups similar in response to continental climate
				Macrogroup	Biogeographic species groups similar in response to regional climate
				Group	Biogeographic species groups similar in response to regional climate & soils
FLORISTIC	Alliance	Species in the dominant layer	LOWER	Alliance	Species mostly in the dominant layer; common species in all layers
	Association	Species in all layers		Association	Species in all layers

strongly on "bottom-up" criteria developed from considerable existing information at the USNVC Association level than were the former hierarchy units, it is expected that they will also provide map classes that relate more directly to lower hierarchy USNVC ecological classes. The USNVC revision also requires a peer review process to establish definitive content (individual units) of all levels of the USNVC. This peer review process currently is in its infancy.

Beginning in 2008, the National Park Service and the interagency LANDFIRE project cooperated to sponsor development of initial content of two of the middle levels of the revised USNVC (Group and Macrogroup) (Faber-Langendoen et al. 2010). Development of content for most of the eastern United States and for most upland vegetation in the western United States was accomplished from 2008 to 2010. Content for USNVC middle levels in the Great Plains, wetland and riparian vegetation in the western United States, and lithomorphic (rock outcrop, talus, sand dune) and cryomorphic (cold-dominated - polar and alpine) vegetation was developed from 2009 to 2011. It is expected that development of content for Alaska will be completed by the end of 2011. Areas of the United States that remain to be addressed are Pacific Islands (including Hawaii, Guam, American Samoa, and Saipan), and the Caribbean region (including tropical Florida, Puerto Rico, and the United States Virgin Islands). As it starts to appear following peer review, new middle level content will be made available to the public in 2011, at http://usnvc.org.

Following the issuance of the standard, the Subcommittee and ESA Panel cooperatively developed an implementation plan for federal and Panel oversight of the content of the USNVC. Since 2008, funding contributions by federal FGDC partners, particularly by the U. S. Forest Service and the U. S. Geological Survey, toward institutionalizing the USNVC, has increased, and a federal USNVC manager position was established.

A.4 Relationship of NPS Vegetation Inventory to the National Vegetation Classification Enterprise

A.4.1 Vegetation and Map Classes
The Federal standard for vegetation classification (Federal Geographic Data Committee 2008) requires "all federal vegetation classification efforts to meet core data requirements that are the same across all federal agencies to permit aggregation of data from all federal agencies" and "that vegetation mapping and inventory units cross walk to the USNVC. This means that the composition of any map unit or inventory unit can be described in terms of one or more vegetation types at an appropriate level of the USNVC hierarchy" (Federal Geographic Data Committee 2008).

The standard does not "preclude alternative classification approaches and systems that address particular needs of Federal agencies" and "should not hamper local federal efforts from doing whatever they need to meet their specific purposes, such as inventory, monitoring, and mapping."

Rather, the standard requires that "when Federal efforts [in vegetation classification and mapping] are conducted, they are conducted in ways that, whatever else they do, they provide the minimum data needed to integrate plot data and cross walk vegetation types, and map units to the content standard (the [US] NVC). Individual plots should be assignable to one vegetation type at the lowest possible level of the NVC hierarchy. Local vegetation types and map units may cross walk to one or more NVC vegetation types at a similar level of the NVC hierarchy."

A.4.2 Classification Plots
By policy, the NPS Vegetation Inventory makes as much data as possible publicly available to fulfill policy and legal mandates, including those that require or encourage development of the USNVC (Federal Geographic Data Committee 2008). In the long run, classification plot data collected from park projects, combined in a comprehensive data set with more geographically extensive data, will be the most significant contribution by the NPS to national standards development and to local, regional, and national scale coordinated vegetation inventories. Currently, park project data are served from the NPS web site

(http://science.nature.nps.gov/im/inventory/veg.cfm). Additionally, Vegbank (http://vegbank.org) (Ecological Society of America Panel. 2008) provides the plots database specified by the NVCS (Federal Geographic Data Committee 2008). At this time the Federal Geographic Data Committee has not determined whether residence in an FGDC central database or in a compatible agency maintained database linked to an FGDC central database will be required for plots used for USNVC development. Plots collected by NPS projects are addressed in more detail in other guidance. At the very least, they must meet the minimal requirements for data quality and completeness and for availability that are specified by the Federal Geographic Data Committee (2008), but need not meet all recommendations. Specific methods for NPS projects are addressed in Lea et al. (2011).

Appendix B: Glossary of Terms, Definitions, and Acronyms
(adapted, in part from Federal Geographic Data Committee 2008)

Abiotic
Pertaining to the nonliving parts of an ecosystem, such as soil, bedrock, air, and water (Helms 1998). *cf.* Biotic.

Alliance
A vegetation classification unit containing one or more Associations, with a defined by a characteristic range of species composition, habitat conditions, 1872 physiognomy, and diagnostic species, typically at least one of which is found in the upper most or dominant stratum of the vegetation (Jennings et al.2009).

Association
A vegetation classification unit defined on the basis of a characteristic range of species composition, diagnostic species occurrence, habitat conditions, and physiognomy (Jennings et al. 2009).

Biotic
Pertaining to the living parts of an ecosystem, such as plants, animals, bacteria, fungi, protists, etc. *cf.* Abiotic.

Canopy
The natural spread of foliage of plants.

Canopy Cover
The percentage of ground covered by the vertical projection of the outermost perimeter of the natural spread of foliage of plants. Small openings in the canopy are included (Society for Range Management 1989, Natural Resources Conservation Service 1997). *cf.* Foliar Cover.

Character species (Characteristic species)
A species that shows a distinct maximum concentration (quantitatively and by presence) in a well-definable vegetation types, sometimes recognized at local, regional, and absolute geographic scales (Mueller-Dombois and Ellenberg 1974, Bruelheide 2000). A character species need not be confined nor even largely confined, to the type of which it is characteristic. *cf.* Differential Species, Fidelity.

Classification
The grouping of similar types (in this case – vegetation types) according to criteria (in this case - physiognomic and floristic) (Federal Geographic Data Committee 2008)

Classification Plot Record
A plot record that contains the data necessary to inform the classification, description, and/or diagnosis of the floristically-derived vegetation types. Such plots typically contain high quality data on floristic composition and structure, and conform to the standard articulated in Jennings et al. (2009). *cf.* Occurrence Plot Records.

Community
In the context of vegetation science, vegetation occupying a specific area on the Earth's surface that is internally homogeneous (the entire stand is classified as a single vegetation type). A community is a real, observable entity, as opposed to a community type, which is an abstraction used to describe communities.

Community Type
In the context of vegetation science, an abstract class unit that is applied to

(Vegetation Type) **(Type)**	a set of [real] plant communities that are related to one another according to a formal taxonomic scheme and that have some common and, often, defining attributes. The term often is applied as being synonymous with the finest level of a classification scheme (e.g., the Association of the U.S. National Vegetation Classification). However, it can be applied more generically to a class value representing any level of a vegetation taxonomy.
Complex	In vegetation mapping, a map class that is intended to represent more than one distinct vegetation type. The individual vegetation types may be either too thematically too finely resolved to map (a thematic complex) or too spatially too finely resolved to map or to map efficiently (a mosaic complex).
Constancy	The percentage of sample units (e.g., plots) in a given data set in which a taxon (e.g., a species) occurs (Jennings et al. 2009). *cf.* Frequency.
Constant species	Species that are present in a high percentage of the plots that define a type, often defined as those species with at least 60% constancy (Mueller-Dombois and Ellenberg 1974).
Continuous Variable	A random variable with an infinite set of outcomes.
Cover	See Canopy Cover, Foliar Cover.
Cross Walk	To describe and document the relationships between members of one set or series and members of another set or series. These relationships may be one-to-one, one-to-many, or many-to-many.
Cultural Vegetation	Vegetation with a distinctive structure, composition, and development determined by regular human activity (Küchler 1969).
Diagnosis	The process of identifying or distinguishing one class in a classification or taxonomy from all other classes. *cf.* Classification.
Diagnostic Species	Any species or group of species whose relative constancy or abundance differentiates one vegetation type from all others (Jennings et al. 2009). It is usually relatively constant and has relatively high fidelity to the type of which it is diagnostic. (Note: in some references, the term "diagnostic species" has also been used to indicate species that tend to indicate certain environmental conditions).
Differential Species	A species that is distinctly more widespread or successful in one of a pair of vegetation types than in the other, although it may be even more successful in other types not under discussion (Curtis 1959, Bruelheide 2000). Differential species are diagnostic species within a limited context of the types being differentiated (as in a single couplet within a diagnostic field key), and can be said to be "situationally diagnostic." *cf.* Character Species, Diagnostic Species, Fidelity.
Dominance	The extent to which a given taxon or growth form has a strong influence in

a community because of its size, abundance, or cover. (Lincoln et al. 1998).

Dominant Species
Species with the highest percent of cover, usually in the uppermost dominant layer (in other contexts dominant species can be defined in terms of biomass, density, height, coverage, etc. (Kimmins 1997).

Ecological Superspecies
In the context of this document, a group of two or more individual plant species that share very similar ecological requirements and that therefore can be treated as vicariants of one another for purposes of identifying or diagnosing vegetation types.

Unlike superspecies, as defined in plant taxonomy, the individual species (the ecological vicariants) that comprise an ecological superspecies need not be (and typically are not) closely related to one another. Also, ecological superspecies are context-dependent; the individual species that comprise an ecological superspecies may serve as a logical diagnostic group in some settings and/or some levels of a hierarchical classification, but not for others.

In the context of the following condition in a diagnostic field key, "the combined absolute cover of both sweet gum (*Liquidambar styraciflua*) and chinquapin oak (*Quercus muehlenbergii*) is less than or equal to the combined absolute cover of both water oak (*Quercus nigra*) and cherrybark oak (*Quercus pagoda*)," the individual species sweet gum and chinquapin oak are vicariants of each other and together comprise one ecological superspecies, and water oak and cherrybark oak are vicariants of each other and together comprise another ecological superspecies. See Ecological Vicariant.

Ecological Vicariant
In the context of this document, the individual species that comprise an ecological superspecies. See Ecological Superspecies.

Ecotone
In vegetation ecology, a transition zone between two different plant communities that occur adjacent to each other and that usually have attributes of both communities.

It is worth pointing out that, in the context of most vegetation classifications (e.g., the USNVC), an "ecotone" has no logical meaning, since vegetation classifications attempt to assign any possible sample unit of vegetation (e.g., stands) of vegetation to a single discrete class (either with certainty or, at least with higher probability than to other classes). An ecotone may be thought of as a phenomenon that exists in nature (i.e., a physical area on the ground), but not in the model chosen to describe that nature, because the model is intended to be an idealized abstraction of nature.

Epiphyte
A vascular or nonvascular plant that colonizes and grows on other plants and does not root on the ground (e.g., Spanish-moss (*Tillandsia usneoides*), resurrection fern (*Pleopeltis polypodioides*), mistletoes (e.g., *Phoradendron*, *Arceuthobium*), various lichens (*Bryoria* spp., *Letharia* spp., *Usnea* spp.).

Fidelity	The degree to which a species is confined in a given vegetation type. The fidelity of a species determines whether it can be considered a **differential** or **character** species, or just a companion (a species not particularly restricted to any vegetation type) or **accidental** species (a species not normally occurring in a particular vegetation type or habitat), (Bruelheide 2000, Lincoln et al. 1998).
Field Stratum	See Herb Stratum
Floating Aquatic Stratum	The layer of vegetation consisting of rooted or drifting plants that float on the water surface; e.g. duckweed, water-lily (Jennings et al. 2009).
Frequency	Percentage of occurrence of a species in a series of subsamples of uniform size contained in a single stand (Daubenmire 1968) or in a single sample unit (e.g., a vegetation subplot or microplot within a larger macroplot or a single point along a point intercept transect). *cf.* Constancy.
Foliar Cover	The percentage of ground covered by the vertical projection of the aerial portion of plants. Small openings in the canopy and intraspecific overlap are excluded (Society for Range Management 1989) *cf.* Canopy Cover.
Forb	A non-aquatic, non-graminoid herb with relatively broad leaves and/or showy flowers. Includes both flowering and spore-bearing, non-graminoid herbs. *cf.* Graminoid.
Graminoid	A non-aquatic, flowering herb with relatively long, narrow leaves and inconspicuous flowers with parts reduced to bracts. Includes grasses, sedges, rushes, and arrowgrasses. *cf.* Forb.
Growth form	The shape or appearance of a plant reflecting growing conditions and genetics. Growth form is usually consistent within a species, but may vary under extremes of environment (Mueller-Dombois and Ellenberg1974). Growth forms determine the visible structure or physiognomy of plant communities (Whittaker 1973).
Ground Stratum	Equivalent to Nonvascular Stratum.
Habitat	A general term referring to the locality, site and particular type of local environment occupied by an organism or community (adapted from Lincoln et al. 1998).
Herb	A vascular plant without perennial aboveground woody stems, with perennating buds borne at or below the ground surface (Whittaker 1975, Federal Geographic Data Committee 1997). Includes forbs (both flowering forbs and spore-bearing ferns), graminoids, and herbaceous vines.
Herb Stratum (Herb Layer) (Field Stratum)	The layer of vegetation consisting of herbs, regardless of height, as well as woody plants less than 0.5 m in height. Equivalent to Field Stratum (Jennings et al. 2009).

Hydromorphic	Pertaining to plants having structural or functional adaptations for living in water-dominated or aquatic habitats (adapted from Federal Geographic Data Committee 1997 and Lincoln et al. 1998).
Inclusion	Distinct vegetation community whose extent is less than the minimum mapping unit.
Indicator Species	A species whose presence, abundance, or vigor is considered to indicate certain site conditions (Gabriel and Talbot 1984).
Inference Area	The elements to be studied or described in a given experiment. In the case of accuracy assessment, the population represents the totality of all errors. Equivalent to sampling population or population (in a statistical sense).
Land Cover	The observed (bio)physical cover of the earth's surface (Di Gregorio and Jansen 1996).
Land Use	The arrangements, activities, and inputs people undertake in a certain land cover type to produce, change, or maintain it (Di Gregorio and Jansen 1996).
Layer (vegetation)	As used in the NPS Vegetation Inventory, equivalent to Stratum.
Liana	A woody, climbing plant that begins life as terrestrial seedlings but relies on external structural support for height growth during some part of its life (Gerwing 2004), typically exceeding 5 m in height or length at maturity.
Lithomorphic	Pertaining to plants or plant-like organisms (e.g., lichens) having structural or functional adaptations for living on rock surfaces or in rocky substrates (i.e. particle sizes larger than 2 mm diameter (adapted from Lincoln et al. 1998)).
Map Class	In a spatial database, a value in a data field for a descriptive categorical attribute that is potentially assigned to a data field for a subset of records in the database. In a vegetation map, a map class might be "ponderosa pine woodland." Equivalent to map unit.
Map Unit	Equivalent to Map Class. Although used as a convention by many in this context, the guidance of the NPS Vegetation Inventory uses the term "map class" rather than "map unit," to refer to a database field value. This avoids linguistic confusion with the term "mapping unit," which refers to a database record. See Map Class.
Mapping Unit	In a spatial database, an individual record (e.g., a polygon, line, or point). This is contrasted with "map class" or "mapping unit" above. In a vegetation map, a mapping unit might be an individual polygon representing a particular stand of a "ponderosa pine woodland."
Metadata	Information about data. This describes the content, quality, condition, and other characteristics of a given dataset. Its purpose is to provide

information about a dataset or some larger data holdings to data catalogues, clearinghouses, and users. Metadata are intended to provide a capability for organizing and maintaining an institution's investment in data as well as to provide information for the application and interpretation of data received through a transfer from an external source (Federal Geographic Data Committee 1997).

Minimum Mapping Unit (MMU)

For a map class vegetation type, the smallest size of a stand of the vegetation type that is represented on a map. Equivalent to minimum map feature of Brewer et al. (2005). For NPS Vegetation Inventory purposes, the minimum mapping unit size is equivalent to the size of the observation area to be used in thematic accuracy assessment. For a minimum mapping unit of 0.5 hectare for a type, it is expected that all vegetation stands that are 0.5 hectare or more in size will be mapped as a distinct and homogeneous vegetation type (exceptions are considered to be mapping errors) and that stands that are less than 0.5 hectare in size may or may not be mapped (if not mapped, they will be treated as inclusions in other map classes and are not considered to be mapping errors).

Mosaic Complex

In vegetation mapping, a map class that is intended to represent more than one distinct vegetation type because the individual vegetation types are spatially too finely resolved to map. The individual types may either be discernable to the mapper (but too small scale to map efficiently) or not discernable. Equivalent to a mosaic-complex in the sense of Mueller-Dombois and Ellenberg (1974). *cf.* Thematic Complex.

National Vegetation Classification Standard (NVCS)

A relatively recently developed standardized scheme for classifying vegetation within the United States. The first version was developed and adopted by the Federal Geographic Data Committee in 1997 (as a variant of the National Vegetation Classification *System* proposed by The Nature Conservancy) and was revised in 2008. As opposed to the more dynamic taxonomic content or database that is prescribed by the standard (the USNVC), the standard itself (NVCS) is a relatively static set of protocols that prescribes the process of development of the USNVC. *cf* United States National Vegetation Classification (USNVC) or National Vegetation Classification (NVC).

Natural Vegetation

Vegetation for which ecological processes primarily determine species and site characteristics; that is, vegetation comprised of a largely spontaneously growing set of plant species that are shaped by both site and biotic processes (Kuchler 1969, Westhoff and Van der Maarel. 1973).

Nonvascular

A plant or plant-like organism without specialized water or fluid conductive tissue (xylem and phloem). Includes mosses, liverworts, hornworts, fungi, lichens, and algae (adapted from Federal Geographic Data Committee 1997).

Nonvascular Stratum (Nonvascular Layer) (Ground Stratum)

The layer of vegetation consisting of non-vascular plants growing on soil or rock surfaces. This includes mosses, liverworts, hornworts, lichens, and algae (Jennings et al. 2009).

Non-vegetated	A category used to classify lands with limited capacity to support life and typically having less than 1 percent vegetative cover. Vegetation, if present, is widely spaced. Typically, the surfaces of non-vegetated areas are sand, freshly exposed rock or subsoil, salt affected soils, human-constructed surfaces, or open water. Subcategories include salt flats; sand dunes; mud flats; beaches; quarries, strip mines, gravel pits, and borrow pits, pavement, and structures (adapted from Natural Resources Inventory 2003). Exceptions include vegetation which exhibits a distinct composition under very sparse conditions (e.g., coastal shore vegetation, playa vegetation, desert pavement vegetation, scree vegetation, some sand dune vegetation). These types often have less than 1% cover.
Observation	Individual members of an inference population that have been selected in a sampling exercise, that are intended to represent that population, and from which variable values are derived to estimate a value for a population parameter. Equivalent to sample unit. Individual observations may have multiple variables assigned to them (e.g., for thematic accuracy assessment, each observation, has, minimally, the variables of map class (sample data identity), vegetation type observed in the field (reference data identity), and a geographic position. Equivalent to Sample Unit.
Observation Area (Observation Plot)	An area associated with an individual sample unit (observation) and its site and over which field (reference) data are collected.
Occurrence Plot Records	Plot records that contain data valuable for ecological and geographical characterization of vegetation, but which do not contain sufficient data to be used in quantitative description of a vegetation type (Jennings et al.2009). *cf.* Classification Plot Records.
Parameter	A numerical population descriptor.
Physiognomy	The visible structure or outward appearance of a plant community as expressed by the dominant growth forms, such as their leaf appearance or deciduousness (Fosberg 1961, Jennings et al. 2009) *cf.* Structure.
Plot	In the context of vegetation classification, an area of defined size and shape that is intended for characterizing a homogenous occurrence of vegetation. *cf.* Relevé.
Polygon	In a spatial database, a record representing a [two-dimensional] area on the Earth's surface that is homogeneous in at least one attribute. In vegetation mapping, a polygon is an abstract representation of a real vegetation stand on the Earth's surface.
Range of Variation	The values of an attribute, such as species composition or environmental parameters, that fall within the upper and lower bounds determined for that attribute. The range of variation in the floristic composition of a vegetation type may, for example, be expressed in terms of its beta diversity (Wilson and Shmida 1984, McCune and Grace 2002), either along an environmental gradient or as the amount of compositional change among a group of plots.

Relevé	A record of vegetation intended for characterizing a stand of vegetation having uniform habitat and relatively homogeneous plant cover, and which is large enough in area to contain a large proportion of the species typically occurring in the plant community type (Mueller-Dombois and Ellenberg 1974) *cf.* Plot.
Sample	A collection of sample units or observations selected together from an inference population for which parameters are estimated. The term sometimes is misapplied to the individual sample units.
Sample Unit	See Observation.
Sampling Population	See Inference Area.
Semi-Natural Vegetation	Vegetation in which past or present human activities significantly influence composition or structure, but do not eliminate or dominate spontaneous ecological processes (Westhoff and Van der Maarel 1973).
Shrub	A woody plant that generally has several erect, spreading, or prostrate stems which give it a bushy appearance. In instances where growth form cannot be determined, woody plants less than 5 m in height at maturity shall be considered shrubs. Includes dwarf shrubs, krummholz, and low or short woody vines (adapted from Federal Geographic Data Committee 1997 and Box 1981).
Stand	A spatially continuous unit of vegetation with uniform composition, structure, and environmental conditions. In the context of vegetation science, essentially synonymous with plant community"
Stratum	In vegetation ecology, a distinct layer comprised of individual plants that share a common height and, often, a common growth form. In sampling theory, a division of an inference population to which a subsample of observations of that population is allocated.
Structure	For vegetation, (1) the spatial pattern of growth forms in a plant community, especially with regard to their height, abundance, or coverage within the individual layers (Gabriel and Talbot 1984). (2) the spatial arrangement of the components of vegetation resulting from plant size and height, vertical stratification into layers, and horizontal spacing of plants (Lincoln et al, 1998, Mueller-Dombois and Ellenberg 1974). *cf.* physiognomy.
Submerged Aquatic Stratum	A layer of vegetation consisting of rooted or drifting plants that by-and-large remain submerged in the water column or on the aquatic bottom; e.g., sea grass (Jennings et al. 2009).
Superspecies	See Ecological Superspecies.
Synthesis Table	A summary table of measures of individual plant species (usually constancy, mean abundance, and range of abundance) for an individual vegetation type. The values for the type are derived (synthesized) from

species measures in individual observations (sample units or plots) that have been assigned to the type.

Thematic Complex   In vegetation mapping, a map class that is intended to represent more than one distinct vegetation type because the individual vegetation types are thematically too finely resolved to map. *cf.* Mosaic Complex.

Tree   A woody plant that generally has a single main stem and a more or less definite crown. In instances where growth form cannot be determined, woody plants equal to or greater than 5 m in height at maturity are generally considered trees (adapted from Federal Geographic Data Committee 1997). Includes dwarf trees (Tart et al. 2005) or "treelets" (Box 1981).

Tree Stratum
(Tree layer)   The layer of vegetation consisting of woody plants more than 5 m in height, including mature trees, shrubs over 5 m tall, and lianas. Epiphytes growing on these woody plants are also included in this stratum (Jennings et al. 2009).

Type   See Community Type.

United States National Vegetation Classification (USNVC) (= National Vegetation Classification (NVC))   The dynamic, and currently somewhat provisional, taxonomic content that is prescribed by the National Vegetation Classification Standard (NVCS). This content currently resides at http://www.usnvc.org and at http://www.natureserve.org/explorer. The standard itself is a relatively static set of protocols that prescribes the process of development of the USNVC. *cf* National Vegetation Classification Standard (NVCS).

Variable   A specific value for a parameter.

Vegetation   The collective plant cover of an area (Federal Geographic Data Committee 1997).

Vegetation type   See Community Type.

Vicariant   See Ecological Vicariant.

Appendix C: Examples of Vegetation Descriptions:

EXHIBIT 1: VEGETATION DESCRIPTION, LITTLE BIGHORN BATTLEFIELD NATIONAL MONUMENT (adapted from Rice et al. in prep.)

Chokecherry Shrubland

USNVC CLASS	Shrubland and Grassland
USNVC SUBCLASS	Temperate and Boreal Shrubland and Grassland
USNVC FORMATION	Temperate Grassland, Meadow, and Shrubland
USNVC DIVISION	Great Plains Grassland and Shrubland
USNVC MACROGROUP	Northern Great Plains Woodland
USNVC GROUP	Great Plains Wooded Draw and Ravine Group
USNVC ALLIANCE	*Prunus virginiana* Shrubland Alliance
USNVC ASSOCIATION	*Prunus virginiana – (Prunus americana)* Shrubland
UNIQUE IDENTIFIER	CEGL001108
LOCAL NAME	Chokecherry Shrubland
MAP CLASS NAME	Chokecherry Shrubland (1:1)

RANGE
Little Bighorn Battlefield National Monument
At Little Bighorn Battlefield National Monument, this shrubland is known only from the Main Unit, where it is found in small patches, primarily on the floodplain of the Little Bighorn River, and also in upland draws.

Global
This Association is a widespread, if small-patch, shrubland that is known from the Columbia Plateau of eastern Washington, eastern Oregon, eastern Nevada, southeastern Idaho, and throughout Wyoming, Montana, Colorado and western South Dakota.

ENVIRONMENTAL DESCRIPTION
Little Bighorn Battlefield National Monument
Stands are found on the floodplain of the Little Bighorn River on Quaternary alluvium (Haverson and Glenberg soils) and in wooded draws in upland settings (mapped mostly as Midway silty clay loams on the Judith River Formation).

Global
This is a widespread small-patch shrubland that is known from the Columbia Plateau of eastern Washington, eastern Oregon, eastern Nevada, southeastern Idaho, and throughout Wyoming, Montana, Colorado and western South Dakota. It occurs in the foothills and lower slopes of mountains, along higher creeks, and in draws and ravines of plateaus and the Great Plains. The elevation range is 716 to 2652 meters (2234-8700 feet). This Association grows at the interface between larger riparian areas and the adjacent upland, as well as on high ridges where snow collects, and occurs as small dense thickets, narrow bands, or irregular patches. It often occupies draws, ephemeral creeks in steep narrow-bottomed canyons, and shallow ravines. It can occur on slopes below seeps and springs. Stands can also occur as small pockets on higher terraces or as narrow bands along the high-water mark of steep banks and incised channels. It also grows at the

base of cliffs adjacent to rivers. Slope varies from flat to very steep, with variable aspects, and can be associated with rock outcrops and talus. Stands are typically on very well-drained, rocky soils but occasionally have finer soils. Soil texture ranges from sandy loam to clay loam.

VEGETATION DESCRIPTION
Little Bighorn Battlefield National Monument
Chokecherry (*Prunus virginiana*) is the dominant species, ranging from fairly open to dense cover. In the upland (draw) "phase," western snowberry (*Symphoricarpos occidentalis*) may be associated with *P. virginiana*. The herbaceous cover is variable, and may be very high when *P. virginiana* cover is patchy to very low. Western wheatgrass (*Pascopyrum smithii*) and Kentucky bluegrass (*Poa pratensis*) are the highest cover species. In the floodplain phase, scattered short trees of green ash (*Fraxinus pennsylvanica*), boxelder (*Acer negundo*), and/or peachleaf willow (*Salix amygdaloides*) may occur, and *Symphoricarpos occidentalis*, silver buffaloberry (*Shepherdia argentea*), Woods' rose (*Rosa woodsii*), and the non-native Russian olive (*Eleagnus angustifolia*) may be associated shrubs. The herbaceous layer in the floodplain "phase" is similarly variable to the "upland" phase, but floristically quite different, with the non-native grasses smooth brome (*Bromus inermis*) and *Poa pratensis* and the native Canada goldenrod (*Solidago canadensis*) and cleavers (*Galium aparine*) characteristic. Vines, including riverbank grape (*Vitis riparia*), eastern poison-ivy (*Toxicodendron radicans*), and western white clematis (*Clematis ligusticifolia*) often contribute substantial cover.

MOST ABUNDANT SPECIES

STRATUM	SPECIES
Tree	*Fraxinus pennsylvanica*
Shrub	*Prunus virginiana, Symphoricarpos occidentalis*
Herbaceous	*Poa pratensis*

CHARACTERISTIC SPECIES
Prunus virginiana

Global
Shrub cover ranges from 100% to more open stands of 30%, with the higher values tending to occur in sites located in drainage bottoms and on lowermost slopes, and the lower values on higher slopes. Chokechery (*Prunus virginiana*) is usually the dominant shrub species, but American wild plum (*Prunus americana*) may be solely present to codominant. Stands can be dominated by one species but are often a mix of three to six other shrub species, which can be as abundant and sometimes more abundant than the two *Prunus* species. Other shrubs include skunkbush sumac (*Rhus trilobata*), golden currant (*Ribes aureum*), prickly currant (*Ribes lacustre*), western gooseberry (*Ribes inerme*), narrowleaf willow (*Salix exigua*), elderberries (*Sambucus* spp.), serviceberries (*Amelanchier* spp.), leadplant (*Amorpha canescens*), big sagebrush (*Artemisia tridentata*), mountain snowberry (*Symphoricarpos oreophilus*), western snowberry (*Symphoricarpos occidentalis*), Rocky Mountain juniper (*Juniperus scopulorum*), Woods' rose (*Rosa woodsii*), creeping barberry (*Mahonia repens*), and poison-ivy (*Toxicodendron* spp). In drainage bottom situations, herbaceous cover is usually sparse, less than 10%. On slopes, the shrubs typically occur in a matrix of other shrubland or grassland types, and graminoid cover can be greater than 75%. Herbaceous species include mountain brome (*Bromus*

marginatus), starry false lily-of-the-valley (*Maianthemum stellatum* (= *Smilacina stellata*)), Kentucky bluegrass (*Poa pratensis*), muttongrass (*Poa fendleriana*), mountain muhly (*Muhlenbergia montana*), basin wildrye (*Leymus cinereus*), nettleleaf giant hyssop (*Agastache urticifolia*), arrowleaf balsamroot (*Balsamorhiza sagittata*), and sulphur-flower buckwheat (*Eriogonum umbellatum*). Exotic herbaceous species may be present, including Canada thistle (*Cirsium arvense*), smooth brome (*Bromus inermis*), and cheatgrass (*Bromus tectorum*).

CLASSIFICATION COMMENTS

The distinction between mesic shrublands *Prunus virginiana - (Prunus americana)* Shrubland and the *Symphoricarpos occidentalis* Shrubland) is somewhat "artificial" at Little Bighorn Battlefield National Monument. *Prunus virginiana* and *Symphoricarpos occidentalis* show a considerable amount of ecological overlap with each other and exhibit considerable small-scale patch (clonal) dominance in both upland draws and on the Little Bighorn floodplain. In matching stands by dominant species to the best USNVC fit, this treatment finds both types splits both types somewhat artificially, with each type exhibiting variable associates, especially in the herbaceous layer, depending on its environmental setting. The dominance of one species over the other, especially on the Little Bighorn floodplain, where grazing by cattle occurs, may relate to selective grazing pressure, as well as ecological site effects. Both USNVC analogs describe both types as an upland draw or floodplain edge vegetation. A more ecologically meaningful treatment might recognize an (1) upland draw type characterized by variable dominance of the two shrub species (with *S. occidentalis* usually at higher cover) and mesic grassland associates (e.g., *Pascopyrum smithii*) and (2) a floodplain type characterized by variable dominance of the two shrub species (with *P. virginiana* usually at higher cover) and more floodplain associates (e.g., *Solidago canadensis*). In the absence of plot data, the USNVC treatment, and the reasonably high accuracy in mapping solely by the dominant shrub species in the stand, we retain this artificial distinction between the two types at Little Bighorn Battlefield National Monument.

EXHIBIT 2: VEGETATION DESCRIPTION, LITTLE BIGHORN BATTLEFIELD NATIONAL MONUMENT (adapted from Rice et al. in prep.)

Weedy Annual Great Plains Herbaceous Vegetation

USNVC CLASS	Shrubland and Grassland
USNVC SUBCLASS	Temperate and Boreal Shrubland and Grassland
USNVC FORMATION	Temperate Grassland, Meadow, and Shrubland
USNVC DIVISION	Great Plains Grassland and Shrubland
USNVC MACROGROUP	Undefined
USNVC GROUP	Undefined
USNVC ALLIANCE	Undefined
USNVC ASSOCIATION	Undefined
UNIQUE IDENTIFIER	NPSLIBI001 (described from this project)
LOCAL NAME	Weedy Annual Great Plains Herbaceous Vegetation
MAP CLASS NAME	Weedy Annual Great Plains Herbaceous Vegetation (1:1)

RANGE
Little Bighorn Battlefield National Monument
At Little Bighorn Battlefield National Monument, this vegetation was mapped in small patches in both units, usually near roads.

Global
This range of this vegetation is not known.

ENVIRONMENTAL DESCRIPTION
Little Bighorn Battlefield National Monument
This type is probably generally distributed throughout Little Bighorn Battlefield National Monument, especially in the headquarters area and along roads. It occurs in areas of anthropogenic soil disturbance, such as roadsides, pathways, waste sites, and maintenance areas, usually occurs in small patches (< 0.5 ha). The largest stand seen was at a maintenance area ("boneyard") that was being re-vegetated (perennial species were not yet established).

Global
Similar vegetation likely occurs in a variety of open disturbed habitats, throughout the Great Plains.

VEGETATION DESCRIPTION
Little Bighorn Battlefield National Monument
(based on 2 accuracy assessment observations)
This type is characterized by a dominance of weedy, mostly non-native, mostly low-growing, annual species. Cover and species composition may be variable and subject to time since disturbance and chance events of colonization and seed banks. Field brome (*Bromus arvensis* (= *Bromus japonicus*)), tall tumblemustard (*Sisymbrium altissimum*), field bindweed (*Convolvulus*

arvensis), cheatgrass (Bromus *tectorum*), smooth brome (*Bromus inermis*), and clasping pepperweed (*Lepidium perfoliatum*) were the most frequent species in the few observed stands.

MOST ABUNDANT SPECIES
STRATUM   SPECIES
Herbaceous   *Bromus arvensis (= Bromus japonicus), Sisymbrium altissimum, Convolvulus arvensis, Bromus tectorum*

CHARACTERISTIC SPECIES
Convolvulus arvensis, Bromus tectorum

Global
The composition of this vegetation is likely highly variable and dependent in part on the breadth or narrowness of the classification treatment.

CLASSIFICATION COMMENTS
Classification of ruderal, semi-natural vegetation at Alliance and Association levels is very under-developed in the USNVCS. This vegetation was mapped as unclassifiable from any existing floristic descriptions. It was determined to the lowest determinable level of the NVCS (the Formation, as defined by the 1997 standard) and given a provisional (project-specific description) as a "placeholder" to classify mapped stands for the Little Bighorn Battlefield project and as an occurrence record for future work.

EXHIBIT 3: VEGETATION DESCRIPTION, NEW RIVER GORGE NATIONAL RIVER (adapted from Vanderhorst et al. (2007))

Common Name (Park-specific): Riverbank Annuals

USNVC English Name: Creeping Lovegrass - Marsh Seedbox - Yellowseed False Pimpernel - Awned Flatsedge Herbaceous Vegetation
USNVC Scientific Name: *Eragrostis hypnoides - Ludwigia palustris - Lindernia dubia - Cyperus squarrosus* Herbaceous Vegetation

LOCAL INFORMATION

Environmental Description: This Association occurs in small patches and linear zones along the shores of the New River. It occurs in positions within the active channel shelf which are very frequently flooded and submerged for long periods. It occurs on eroded riverbanks and wet beaches and may also occur in back channels and sloughs. The short periods of exposure and heavy disturbance regime result in vegetation dominated by fast-growing annual species. Patches may be highly ephemeral, but this Association will likely persist on the landscape under natural or altered flooding regimes. Substrates are sand or silty sand. In the one sampled plot, pH measured in the field was 6.0. Occurrences may be partially shaded by overhanging trees but are best developed in areas with full solar exposure. They are likely to be scattered throughout the length of the New River in the park with elevations ranging from 244 to 402 meters (760 to 1300 feet).

Vegetation Description: This Association represents herbaceous vegetation dominated by weedy native and exotic annuals and short-lived perennials which occur on the shores of the New River. Overhanging trees in the one sampled plot include eastern sycamore (*Platanus occidentalis*) and silver maple (*Acer saccharinum*). There are seedlings and young saplings of river birch (*Betula nigra*) in the plot. Herbaceous cover in the plot when sampled was 60%. Characteristic herbs include common threeseed mercury (*Acalypha rhomboidea*), spreading sandmat (*Chamaesyce humistrata*), Mexican tea (*Chenopodium ambrosioides*), strawcolored flatsedge (*Cyperus strigosus*), smooth crabgrass (*Digitaria ischaemum*), Virginia buttonweed (*Diodia virginiana*), barnyardgrass (*Echinochloa crus-galli*), crested latesummer mint (*Elsholtzia ciliata*), creeping lovegrass (*Eragrostis hypnoides*), American burnweed (*Erechtites hieraciifolia*), slender fimbry (*Fimbristylis autumnalis*) ground ivy (*Glechoma hederacea*), dwarf Saint Johnswort (*Hypericum mutilum*) whitegrass (*Leersia virginica*), yellowseed false pimpernel (*Lindernia dubia* var. *dubia*), Nepalese stilt grass (*Microstegium vimineum*), common yellow oxalis (*Oxalis stricta*), fall panicgrass (*Panicum dichotomiflorum*), Gattinger's panicgrass (*Panicum gattingeri* (= *Panicum philadelphicum* ssp. *gattingeri*), Oriental lady's thumb (*Polygonum cespitosum* var. *longisetum*), West Indian nightshade (*Solanum ptychanthum*), common mullein (*Verbascum thapsus*), and white vervain (*Verbena urticifolia*). Vascular plant species richness in the single sampled plot is 31.

Most Abundant Species: Information not available.

Characteristic Species: *Acalypha rhomboidea, Chamaesyce humistrata, Chenopodium ambrosioides, Cyperus strigosus, Digitaria ischaemum, Diodia virginiana, Echinochloa crus-galli, Elsholtzia ciliata, Eragrostis hypnoides, Erechtites hieraciifolia, Fimbristylis autumnalis, Glechoma hederacea, Hypericum mutilum, Leersia virginica, Lindernia dubia* var. *dubia, Microstegium vimineum, Oxalis stricta, Panicum dichotomiflorum, Panicum gattingeri,*

Polygonum cespitosum var. *longisetum, Solanum ptychanthum, Verbascum thapsus, Verbena urticifolia*

Other Noteworthy Species:
Other Noteworthy Species: Information not available.
Subnational Distribution with Cross Walk data:

State	State Rank	Confidence	State Name	Reference
WV	SNR	.	[not cross walked]	.

Local Range: This Association is likely to occur in small patches along the shores of the New River throughout its length in the park.

Classification Comments: Many of the annual species which characterize this Association are also common in *Salix nigra - Betula nigra / Schoenoplectus (pungens, tabernaemontani)* Wooded Herbaceous Vegetation (CEGL006463) and *Peltandra virginica - Saururus cernuus - Boehmeria cylindrica / Climacium americanum* Herbaceous Vegetation (CEGL007696), and distinction among these types may depend on the size of the sampled patch. Because it occurs in very small, potentially ephemeral patches, it is recognized as an Association which occurs in the park, but no attempt was made to map individual patches.

Other Comments:
Other Comments: Information not available.
Local Description Authors: J.P. Vanderhorst
Plots: NERI.326.
New River Gorge National River Inventory Notes:
New River Gorge National River Inventory Notes: Information not available.

GLOBAL INFORMATION

USNVC CLASSIFICATION

USNVC Class	Shrubland and Grassland
USNVC Subclass	Temperate and Boreal Shrubland and Grassland
USNVC Formation	Temperate and Boreal Freshwater Wet Meadow and Marsh
USNVC Division	Eastern North America Freshwater Wet Meadow, Riparian, and Marsh
USNVC Macrogroup	Eastern River Scour Wetland
USNVC Group	Eastern River Scour Group
USNVC Alliance	*Eragrostis hypnoides - Lipocarpha micrantha - Micranthemum umbrosum* Seasonally Flooded Herbaceous Alliance (A.1816)
USNVC Alliance (English)	Creeping Lovegrass - Small-flower Hemicarpha - Shaded Mudflower Seasonally Flooded Herbaceous Alliance
USNVC Association	*Eragrostis hypnoides - Ludwigia palustris - Lindernia dubia - Cyperus squarrosus* Herbaceous Vegetation
USNVC Association (English) Identifier	Creeping Lovegrass - Marsh Seedbox - Yellowseed False Pimpernel - Awned Flatsedge Herbaceous Vegetation
USNVC Identifier	CEGL006483
Map Class Name	Steep Riparian Edge (1:10)
Ecological System(s)	Central Appalachian Riparian (CES202.609)

GLOBAL DESCRIPTION

Concept Summary: This Association occurs along major rivers in the Piedmont and mountains of Maryland, Virginia, West Virginia, and the District of Columbia. It occupies the lowest parts of riverbanks or very low rivershore depositional bars in areas that receive essentially full sunlight. These habitats are inundated for most of the winter and spring and are generally consistently exposed only from early summer to early autumn (i.e., the "drawdown" zone). During wet years they may be nearly continuously inundated. The type usually occurs as a narrow strip (frequently <2 m wide) along the shoreline. This Association may also develop, sometimes as very large (>1 ha) patches, on the drawdown shores and seasonally exposed islands of impounded rivers. Vegetation of stands varies from sparse to dense (10-80% cover) and is characterized by low-growing mats of predominantly annual species, with some low, fast-growing perennials also present. Creeping lovegrass (*Eragrostis hypnoides*), marsh seedbox (*Ludwigia palustris),* yellowseed false pimpernel (*Lindernia dubia var. dubia*), and bearded flatsedge (*Cyperus squarrosus*) are constant and often abundant. Other characteristic annuals (and biennials) are common threeseed mercury (*Acalypha rhomboidea*), valley redstem (*Ammannia coccinea*), sweet sagewort (*Artemisia annua*), devil's beggartick (*Bidens frondosa),* sandmats (*Chamaesyce humistrata* and *Chamaesyce maculata*), Mexican tea (*Chenopodium ambrosioides*), slender flatsedge (*Cyperus bipartitus*), fragrant flatsedge (*Cyperus odoratus*), Virginia buttonweed (*Diodia virginiana*), barnyardgrass (*Echinochloa crus-galli*), crested latesummer mint (*Elsholtzia ciliata*), false daisy (*Eclipta prostrata*), sandbar lovegrass (*Eragrostis frankii*), dwarf Saint Johnswort (*Hypericum mutilum*), yellowseed false pimpernel (*Lindernia dubia* var. *dubia* and var. *anagallidea*), smallflower halfchaff sedge (*Lipocarpa micrantha*), green carpetweed (*Mollugo verticillata*), fall panicgrass (*Panicum dichotomiflorum*), Gattinger's panicgrass (*Panicum gattingeri* (= *Panicum philadelphicum* ssp. *gattingeri*), horsetail paspalum (*Paspalum fluitans*), Oriental lady's thumb (*Polygonum cespitosum* var. *longisetum*), Fernald's yellowcress (*Rorippa palustris* ssp. *fernaldiana*), lowland rotala (*Rotala ramosior*), West Indian nightshade (*Solanum ptychanthum*), and rough cocklebur (*Xanthium strumarium*).

Frequent perennials include smallspike false-nettle (*Boehmeria cylindrica*), strawcolored flatsedge (*Cyperus strigosus*), whitegrass (*Leersia virginica*), American water-willow (*Justicia americana*), American water horehound (*Lycopus americanus*), sharpwing monkeyflower (*Mimulus alatus*), ditch stonecrop (*Penthorum sedoides*), lanceleaf fogfruit (*Phyla lanceolata*), creeping yellowcress (*Rorippa sylvestris*), and brookweed (*Samolus valerandi* ssp. *parviflorus*). Stranded mats of yellow star-grass (*Heteranthera dubia* (= *Zosterella dubia*)) are also frequent. Seedlings of taller annuals and perennials such as halberdleaf rosemallow (*Hibiscus laevis*), thoroughworts (*Eupatorium* spp.), and knotweeds (*Polygonum* spp.) are also frequent but rarely reach full stature. Overhanging trees of eastern sycamore (*Platanus occidentalis*) and silver maple (*Acer saccharinum*) may be present, as well as saplings of river birch (*Betula nigra*).

Environmental Description: Natural occurrences of this community occupy the lowest parts of riverbanks or very low rivershore depositional bars in areas that receive essentially full sunlight. It occurs on eroded riverbanks and wet beaches and may also occur in back channels and sloughs. These habitats are inundated for most of the winter and spring and are generally consistently exposed only from early summer to early autumn (i.e., the "drawdown" zone). During wet years they may be nearly continuously inundated. The type usually occurs as a narrow strip (frequently <2 m wide) along the shoreline. Though more frequently flooded than higher depositional bars that support tall annual or perennial herbaceous vegetation, the habitats

74

of this type probably experience lesser amounts of sediment turnover (erosion and deposition) during a flood of a given magnitude (i.e., are less stochastically disturbed). Soils are usually deep to somewhat shallow sandy loams, loamy sands, or silt loams that are likely saturated to near the surface throughout the growing season. They would likely be classified as Entisols and generally have high pH (7.0), high calcium levels, and are 100% base-saturated. Mean particle size (phi) of samples collected from several Potomac River sites is 2.7 to 1.9. This Association may also develop, sometimes as very large (>1 ha) patches, on the drawdown shores and seasonally exposed islands of impounded rivers, e.g., at the upper end of the John H. Kerr Reservoir on the Roanoke River in Halifax, Mecklenburg, and Charlotte counties, Virginia.

Vegetation Description: With the exception of several semi-aquatic perennial species, the short periods of exposure and heavy disturbance regime select for opportunistic, non-competitive annual species and low, short-lived, fast-growing perennials, all of which can grow and reproduce quickly. It would be expected that many species in this community type have relatively long-lived seedbanks and, possibly, specialized germination requirements. Vegetation of stands varies from sparse to dense (10-80% cover) and is characterized by low-growing mats of predominantly annual species. *Eragrostis hypnoides, Ludwigia palustris, Lindernia dubia var. dubia*, and *Cyperus squarrosus* are constant and often abundant. Other characteristic annuals (and biennials) are *Acalypha rhomboidea, Ammannia coccinea, Artemisia annua, Bidens frondosa, Chamaesyce humistrata, Chamaesyce maculata, Chenopodium ambrosioides, Cyperus bipartitus, Cyperus odoratus, Diodia virginiana, Echinochloa crus-galli, Eclipta prostrata, Elsholtzia ciliata, Eragrostis frankii, Fimbristylis autumnalis, Hypericum mutilum, Lindernia dubia var. anagallidea, Lindernia dubia var. dubia, Lipocarpha micrantha, Mollugo verticillata, Panicum dichotomiflorum var. dichotomiflorum, Panicum gattingeri (= Panicum philadelphicum ssp. gattingeri), Paspalum fluitans, Polygonum caespitosum var. longisetum, Rorippa palustris ssp. fernaldiana, Rotala ramosior, Solanum ptychanthum*, and *Xanthium strumarium*. Frequent perennials include *Boehmeria cylindrica, Cyperus strigosus, Leersia virginica, Justicia americana, Lycopus americanus, Mimulus alatus, Penthorum sedoides, Phyla lanceolata, Rorippa sylvestris*, and *Samolus valerandi ssp. parviflorus*. Stranded mats of *Heteranthera dubia (= Zosterella dubia)* are also frequent. Seedlings of taller annuals and perennials such as *Hibiscus laevis, Eupatorium* spp., and *Polygonum* spp. are also frequent but rarely reach full stature. A variant of this community in the Potomac River drainage is characterized primarily by low, rhizomatous colonies of *Eleocharis tenuis*. Species that are more characteristic of the James River and Roanoke River occurrences in central and southern Virginia include *Cyperus flavicomus, Cyperus erythrorhizos, Ludwigia decurrens, Paspalum dissectum, Rorippa sessiliflora*, and *Sagittaria calycina var. calycina*. Overhanging trees of *Platanus occidentalis* and *Acer saccharinum* may be present, as well as saplings of *Betula nigra*.

Most Abundant Species: Information not available.

Characteristic Species: *Acalypha rhomboidea, Artemisia annua, Chamaesyce humistrata, Chenopodium ambrosioides, Diodia virginiana, Echinochloa crus-galli, Eclipta prostrata, Eragrostis frankii, Eragrostis hypnoides, Fimbristylis autumnalis, Hypericum mutilum, Leersia virginica, Lindernia dubia, Lipocarpha micrantha, Mimulus alatus, Oxalis stricta, Panicum dichotomiflorum, Panicum gattingeri, Polygonum caespitosum var. longisetum, Rotala ramosior, Solanum ptychanthum, Verbascum thapsus, Verbena urticifolia*

Other Noteworthy Species:

Other Noteworthy Species: Information not available.

USFWS Wetland System:

USFWS Wetland System: not applicable

DISTRIBUTION

Range: This community occurs along major rivers in the Piedmont and mountains of Maryland, Virginia, West Virginia, and the District of Columbia. It is definitely known from the Potomac, Shenandoah, Monocacy, New, James, and Roanoke rivers, and likely occurs in other drainages of the region.

States/Provinces: DC, MD, VA, WV

Federal Lands: NPS (C&O Canal National Historical Park, George Washington Memorial Parkway, Harpers Ferry national Historical Park, Monocacy National Battlefield, New River Gorge National River).

CONSERVATION STATUS

Rank: G3 (29-Sep-2006)

Reasons: Although natural stands occur in very small, somewhat ephemeral patches, this type is widely distributed along major rivers in the greater Mid-Atlantic Piedmont and mountain region and is adaptable to artificial drawdown shores, where it sometimes occurs in extensive patches.

CLASSIFICATION INFORMATION

Status: Standard

Confidence: 2 - Moderate

Comments: The classification is supported by analysis of data from 25 plots collected for the National Capital Region Parks project, three plots collected along the Roanoke River in southern Virginia, and one plot from the New River Gorge in West Virginia. Many of the annual species which characterize this Association are also common in *Salix nigra - Betula nigra / Schoenoplectus (pungens, tabernaemontani)* Wooded Herbaceous Vegetation (CEGL006463) and *Peltandra virginica - Saururus cernuus - Carex crinita / Climacium americanum* Herbaceous Vegetation (CEGL007696), and distinction between these types may depend on the size of the sampled patch.

Appendix D: Examples of Field Keys

EXHIBIT 4: VEGETATION FIELD KEY TO VICKSBURG NATIONAL MILITARY PARK
(adapted from Lea et al. in prep.)

Instructions on use of key:

This key is dichotomous and hierarchical. Beginning with couplet 1, the user is directed through a number of couplets, and should select whichever side of the couplet (a or b) fits the vegetation best. The user should read ***both*** sides of the couplet (both a and b) before evaluating and proceeding. At several places in this key, the user is asked to consider multiple (2-4) criteria on each side of the couplet. Where these multiple, independent criteria are to be evaluated, criteria on both sides of the couplet may prove to be correct (i.e., the criteria on each couplet side are not necessarily mutually exclusive). In these cases, the user should evaluate each individual criterion independently from the others, consider all criteria on each side of the couplet, and select the couplet side that ***best*** represents the vegetation before proceeding. Answers to couplets will lead to either another couplet to be evaluated in progression or to a vegetation type (final answer). Note that there may be more than one path through the key to arriving at an individual vegetation type.

In some individual statements, the user is asked to estimate the combined (aggregate) cover of several species. In these cases, one, some or all of the named species may be present. For purposes of estimating cover, these multiple species should be considered a single species; if A and B are both species in such a species aggregate, and a part of the cover of species B is overtopped by part of the cover for species A, this portion of the cover for species B should not be counted.

This key is designed to be used in relatively homogeneous stands of vegetation within Vicksburg National Military Park and to be optimally accurate when vegetation is observed at a scale of 0.25 to 1.0 hectares. It will become progressively less reliable at smaller scales. It may not be reliable outside of Vicksburg National Military Park.

It is expected that users of the key can identify all species named in the key (and potential species with which they may be confused at Vicksburg National Military Park). For users with more limited knowledge of the full flora of this site, the keys will likely work adequately if the user omits evaluating all key criteria (e.g., shrub, vine, and herbaceous species for someone who recognizes only trees) that refer to any species unknown to him/her. Do not use a criterion, if you know some, but not all, individual species named in a single criterion. The key also assumes that the user can estimate plant cover relatively accurately and precisely (repeatably).

Keys are imperfect. It is always a good idea to confirm a final keyed answer by reading the corresponding vegetation description corresponding to the keyed type. If an answer seems implausible, one should re-key the stand, examining other possible couplets from those that were selected the first time through the key.

GLOSSARY OF TERMS USED IN THIS KEY:

Absolute cover: The proportion of an observed area that is underneath (covered by) the canopy of an individual plant species (or a group of plant species). "Underneath" means under the vertical projection down to the ground of the horizontal outline of the foliar crown of the plant species or group of species. Absolute cover is often regarded as the area outlined by the "drip line" of the crown; small openings between branches and leaves within this outline are generally not subtracted from this area in estimating cover. Cover of individuals of the same applicable species (or the same applicable group) that is overtopped by cover of that same species or group is not counted. As an example of how to estimate absolute cover, if the observation area is 0.25 hectare (2,500 square meters), and the canopy of any eastern red cedar (*Juniperus virginiana*) covers an estimated 150 square meters of this area, then the absolute cover of eastern red cedar over this observation area is calculated and recorded as 6% (150 divided by/ 2,500). Absolute cover for an individual species may not exceed 100% for an observation area (or an individual stratum within an observation area), but the combined absolute cover of multiple or all species may exceed 100%.

Relative cover: The proportion of the total of all absolute cover (all species in the observation area or all species within a specified layer in the observation area) area that is comprised of the species or ecological superspecies (species group). If a tree layer is comprised of 40% absolute cover of boxelder (*Acer negundo*), 20% cover of sweet gum (*Acer negundo*) and 20 % cover of American sycamore (*Platanus occidentalis*), then the *relative* cover of boxelder for the observed area is 50% (40% divided by the sum of 40% + 20% + 20%) and the relative cover of the other two species is 25% each. The relative cover for all species for an observation area, or for a specified stratum in an observation area must sum to 100%.

Dominant (dominated by): For purposes of this key, the individual species (or ecological superspecies) having the highest absolute or relative cover (i.e., the plurality of all cover) of any species or superspecies within the observation area.

Layer: A grouping of plants within a vegetation stand that have a similar life form and height range. The layers used in this key are tree, shrub, vine, and herbaceous, with the life form groups are defined individually below. Layer is synonymous with stratum.

Trees: For purposes of this key, woody plants generally more than 5 meters tall and usually have multiple stems only in response to past physical damage to the main stem.

Vines: Woody or herbaceous plants with elongated (e.g., more than 1 meter) aerial stems that are not self-supporting. Vines are supported by other plants or creep on the ground.

Shrubs: For purposes of this key, woody plants generally less than 5 meters tall. Shrubs often produce multiple stems in the absence of physical damage to a main stem.

Herbaceous: Non-woody vascular plant species. For purposes of this key, seedlings of woody species that are less than 0.5 meter tall also are included in the herbaceous layer.

Forbs: For purposes of this key, broad-leaved herbaceous plant species (excludes grasses, sedges, and rushes).

Wetlands: Vegetation types in which wetland plant species (those ranked OBL or FACW on National List of plants that occur in wetlands) have higher total cover than do upland plant species (see below).

Uplands: Vegetation types in which non-wetland plant species (those ranked FAC, FACU, or UPL (not listed) on National List of plants that occur in wetlands) have higher total cover than do wetland plant species (see below).

GENERAL KEY

1a. Vegetation is dominated by trees (absolute cover of all tree species combined is greater than or equal to 25%)...go to couplet 2 (Forests Key)

1b. Vegetation is not dominated by trees (absolute cover of all tree species combined is less than 25%.....................go to couplet 13 (Shrublands and Herbaceous Vegetation Key)

FORESTS KEY (1A)

2a. Combined absolute cover of all evergreen tree species exceeds combined absolute cover of all deciduous tree species. Combined absolute cover of evergreens (loblolly pine (*Pinus taeda*) and/or eastern red cedar (*Juniperus virginiana*)) is greater than or equal to 25%. Vegetation is an open canopy of evergreen trees over a herbaceous layer that is dominated by low (less than 0.5 meters tall) grasses..................................***Pinus taeda* Planted Forest**

2b. Vegetation is not as above. Combined absolute cover of all deciduous tree species exceeds combined absolute cover of all evergreen species. Combined absolute cover of evergreens (loblolly pine (*Pinus taeda*) and/or eastern red cedar (*Juniperus virginiana*)) is less than 25%. Tree layer is closed to partially open. Herbaceous layer dominated by the tall grass giant cane (*Arundinaria gigantea*) or by some mix of grasses and forbs ....go to 3

    3a. Black willow (*Salix nigra*) is the most abundant species in the tree layer................ ....***Salix nigra* Large River Floodplain Forest**

    3b. Not as above. Black willow (*Salix nigra*) is absent or unimportant....................go to 4

        4a. Combined absolute cover of black locust (*Robinia pseudoacacia*) and/or paper mulberry (*Broussonetia papyrifera*) is greater than or equal to 35%...***Robinia pseudoacacia* Forest**

        4b. Combined absolute cover of black locust (*Robinia pseudoacacia*) and/or paper mulberry (*Broussonetia papyrifera*) is less than 35%...............................…......go to 5

            5a. Boxelder (*Acer negundo*) is the most abundant species in the tree layer.......... ....go to 6

                6a Boxelder (*Acer negundo*) has greater than or equal to 40% relative cover (among all trees) and greater than or equal to 40% absolute cover.....…............. ....…................***Acer negundo* Forest**

                6b Either the relative (among all trees) or absolute cover of boxelder (*Acer negundo*), or both, is less than 40%..go to 7

                    7a. Absolute cover of tulip tree (*Liriodendron tulipifera*) is greater than or equal to 25%.. ***Liriodendron tulipifera* / (*Cercis canadensis*) / (*Lindera benzoin*) Forest**

7b. Absolute cover of tulip tree (*Liriodendron tulipifera*) is less than 25%..
***Liquidambar styraciflua - Carya illinoinensis - Quercus nigra* Forest**

5b. A species other than boxelder (*Acer negundo*) has the highest absolute cover of any species in the tree layer...go to 8

8a. Sweet gum (*Liquidambar styraciflua*) has greater than or equal to 50% relative cover and greater than or equal to 60% absolute cover.............go to 9

9a. Absolute cover of tulip tree (*Liriodendron tulipifera*) is greater than or equal to 25%...
***Liriodendron tulipifera / (Cercis canadensis) / (Lindera benzoin)* Forest**

9b. Absolute cover of tulip tree (*Liriodendron tulipifera*) is less than 25%...***Liquidambar styraciflua* Forest**

8b. Sweet gum (*Liquidambar styraciflua*) has less than 50% relative cover or less than 60% absolute cover or both...go to 10

10a. Consider all three of the following criteria:
(1) Absolute cover of tulip tree (*Liriodendron tulipifera*) is greater than or equal to 25%.
(2) Combined absolute cover of American sycamore (*Platanus occidentalis*), pecan (*Carya illinoensis*), and/or water oak (*Quercus nigra*) is less than 20%.
(3) At least three of the following five shrub or herbaceous species are present: northern spicebush (*Lindera benzoin*), wild hydrangea (*Hydrangea arborescens*), oakleaf hydrangea (*Hydrangea quercifolia*), bristly greenbrier (*Smilax tamnoides*), lowland bladder fern (*Cystopteris protrusa*)..
***Liriodendron tulipifera / (Cercis canadensis) / (Lindera benzoin)* Forest**

10b. Consider all three of the following criteria:
1) Absolute cover of tulip tree (*Liriodendron tulipifera*) is less than 25%.
(2) Combined absolute cover of American sycamore (*Platanus occidentalis*), pecan (*Carya illinoensis*), and/or water oak (*Quercus nigra*) is greater than or equal to than 20%.
(3) No more than two of the following five shrub or herbaceous species are present: northern spicebush (*Lindera benzoin*), wild hydrangea (*Hydrangea arborescens*), oakleaf hydrangea (*Hydrangea quercifolia*), bristly greenbrier (*Smilax tamnoides*), lowland bladder fern (*Cystopteris protrusa*)...go to 11

11a. Consider all four of the following criteria:

(1) Combined absolute cover of American sycamore (*Platanus occidentalis*), boxelder (*Acer negundo*), and/or red mulberry (*Morus rubra*) is greater than or equal to 20%.
(2) Combined absolute cover of all oaks (*Quercus* spp.) is less than 40%.
(3) Combined absolute cover of oakleaf hydrangea (*Hydrangea quercifolia*), eastern redbud (*Cercis canadensis*), and/or dogwoods (*Cornus* spp.) is less than 5%.
(4) Jumpseed (*Polygonum virginianum*) and/or common ladyfern (*Athyrium filix-femina*) are present...
***Platanus occidentalis - Liquidambar styraciflua - (Ulmus americana) / (Crataegus viridis)* Forest**

11b. Consider all four of the following criteria:
1) Combined absolute cover of American sycamore (*Platanus occidentalis*), boxelder (*Acer negundo*), and/or red mulberry (*Morus rubra*) is less than 20%.
(2) Combined absolute cover of all oaks (*Quercus* spp.) is greater than or equal to 40%.
 (3) Combined absolute cover of oakleaf hydrangea (*Hydrangea quercifolia*), eastern redbud (*Cercis canadensis*), and/or dogwoods (*Cornus* spp.) is greater than or equal to 5%
(4) Jumpseed (*Polygonum virginianum*) and/or common ladyfern (*Athyrium filix-femina*) are both absent..........................…..…go to 12

12a. The combined absolute cover of both sweet gum (*Liquidambar styraciflua*) and chinquapin oak (*Quercus muehlenbergii*) is greater than the combined absolute cover of both water oak (*Quercus nigra*) and cherrybark oak (*Quercus pagoda*)......................…..
***Liquidambar styraciflua - Carya illinoinensis - Quercus nigra* Forest**

12b. The combined absolute cover of both sweet gum (*Liquidambar styraciflua*) and chinquapin oak (*Quercus muehlenbergii*) is less than or equal to the combined absolute cover of both water oak (*Quercus nigra*) and cherrybark oak (*Quercus pagoda*)……....................***Quercus pagoda - Quercus nigra* Forest**

SHRUBLANDS AND HERBACEOUS VEGETATION KEY (1B)

13a. Vegetation is characterized by shrubs or vines (the absolute cover of all shrub and/or vine species combined is greater than or equal to 35%)....................................go to 14

    14a. The absolute cover of all vine species combined exceeds the absolute cover of all shrub species combined.............................*Pueraria montana* var. *lobata* Vine-Shrubland

    14b. The absolute cover of all shrub species combined is equal to or exceeds the absolute cover of all vine species combined.................................... *Acer negundo* Forest*

13b. Vegetation is characterized by herbaceous vegetation (the absolute cover of all shrub and/or vine species combined is less than 35%)...............................…..………...go to 15

    15a. Either bahiagrass (*Paspalum notatum*) or Johnsongrass (*Sorghum halepense*) has the highest absolute cover among grass species...go to 16

        16a. Bahiagrass (*Paspalum notatum*) has the highest absolute cover among grass species.....................................***Paspalum notatum* Herbaceous Vegetation**

        16b. Johnsongrass (*Sorghum halepense*) has the highest absolute cover among grass species.....................................**.*Sorghum halepense* Herbaceous Vegetation**

    15b. Neither bahiagrass (*Paspalum notatum*) nor Johnsongrass (*Sorghum halepense*) has the highest absolute cover among grass species……………………………….….………
… … … … … … … … … … … ....***Lolium (arundinaceum, pratense)* Herbaceous Vegetation**

        * - shrubby variant of this forest type

EXHIBIT 5: FIELD KEY TO VEGETATION CLASSES OF SHENANDOAH NATIONAL PARK (adapted from Young et al. 2009)

INSTRUCTIONS: The following dichotomous key to the vegetation classes of the Shenandoah National Park Vegetation Map ver. 2.0 was created for use by park natural resource managers and personnel conducting map accuracy assessment. A dichotomous key is a tool for identifying unknown entities, in this case vegetation types. It is structured by a series of couplets, two statements that describe different, mutually exclusive characteristics of the vegetation. The overall key, as well as discrete portions, begin with couplets identifying larger vegetation patterns and groups (*e.g.*, upland vegetation vs. wetland vegetation; see Figure 1) and work progressively toward identifying the finer-scale vegetation types that constitute the map classes. The key is based on a comprehensive quantitative classification of vegetation that was produced for this project, and represents a major revision of the ver. 1.0 key, which was extensively field tested. For convenience, major segments of the key that deal with specific vegetation groups (*e.g.*, "forests and woodlands with > 25% coniferous tree cover" or "vegetation of rock outcrops and nonvascular boulderfields") are identified with bold headers. Environmental information, as well as floristic and structural characteristics, is used in the key. Geology, in particular, is an important variable controlling the distribution of some vegetation types in the Park. It is recommended that users of this key become familiar with the three major geologic suites (metabasaltic, granitic, and metasedimentary) of the northern Blue Ridge and, if necessary, carry a geologic map of the park in the field. To some extent, the use of individual herbaceous species has been reduced by utilizing groups of ecologically similar herbaceous plants (*e.g.*, "mesophytic nutrient-requiring herbs"). The characteristic species of these groups (Table 1), as well as a glossary of some commonly used technical terms, are included at the end of these instructions. The recommended procedure for using this key is to start at the beginning and progressively work through a series of couplets until a satisfactory identification of the vegetation being examined is reached. Once a user is thoroughly familiar with the key through extensive field use, it will often be possible to skip directly to the appropriate, major leg of the key. In most cases, choosing the statement that best fits the vegetation and environmental characteristics in question at each couplet will lead the user to the correct vegetation type. However, it is important to recognize that no key to vegetation is infallible or perfect. Natural vegetation is frequently gradational on the landscape, resulting in stands that are transitional between classified types. In addition, natural or human disturbance may obscure typical characteristics of a vegetation type, and introduce atypical ones. In some cases, it may be necessary to run a stand through two different legs of the key if uncertainties about how to resolve a couplet exist. To make it easier for users to make choices based on the preponderance of evidence, multiple characters (environmental, floristic, and/or structural) are often used in the key. In addition, certain types are redundantly included in two or more legs of the key to account for their natural variability. The dichotomous key should be used in conjunction with the detailed vegetation map class descriptions to confirm that the vegetation type selected with the key is appropriate.

The scale of observation may influence the performance of this key in the field, especially if the assessment of vegetation is based on prescribed observation points within polygons of the vegetation map (e.g., as in accuracy assessment procedures). The key characters may not be accurate in delineating vegetation types unless areas of sufficient size and homogeneity are considered. In forests and woodlands, a minimum of 0.5 hectare (5000 square meters) of contiguous area should be assessed. This represents the minimum map unit size for vegetation under the USGS-NPS vegetation mapping program, and translates into a circle with a 40-meter radius, or a rectangle 50 x 100 meters. In cases where an observation area falls in an ecotone or contains two distinctly different vegetation types, it is essential to observe as large an area as possible in order to determine which type is the prevalent type within the polygon. However, many small-patch community types (primarily wetlands and rock outcrops) may be mapped with polygons less than 0.5 ha. In these cases, assessment of the entire polygon is recommended

GLOSSARY OF SELECTED TECHNICAL TERMS

Co-dominant –pertaining to a plant (usually in the uppermost stratum) that is one of two or more species sharing high cover and abundance in a stand.

Dominant – pertaining to a plant (usually in the uppermost stratum) that has the highest cover and abundance in a stand.

Dry-Mesophytic – descriptor of plants that prefer soil conditions intermediate between dry and moist but well drained; such conditions are widespread on average slopes in the Park.

Early-successional – descriptor for forest vegetation that has regenerated on formerly cleared land; typically consists of fast-growing, light-demanding species which, in time, will be replaced by longer-lived, shade-tolerant species (i.e., *later-successional* vegetation).

Ericad, Ericaceous species – a plant of the Heath Family (*Ericaceae*), e.g., *Kalmia latifolia*, *Rhododendron* spp., *Gaylussacia baccata*, *Vaccinium* spp., *Menziesia pilosa*, *Lyonia ligustrina*.

Forest – vegetation dominated by trees at least 6 meters tall producing a more or less closed canopy, typically with 60-100% cover; some forests may temporarily have < 60% canopy cover following disturbances such as windthrow, disease, etc.

Herb – a vascular plant lacking woody tissue at or above ground level; includes *Forbs* (broad-leaved herbaceous plants) and *Graminoids* (grasses, sedges, and rushes).

Herb layer – the lowest vascular vegetation stratum, including woody plants < 0.5m tall and all herbaceous plants regardless of height.

High-elevation – above 3,000 feet in elevation.

Lithophytic – descriptor of a vascular plant that is confined to, or particularly characteristic of, rock habitats (outcrop crevices, shelves, ledges).

Low-elevation – below 2,000 feet in elevation.

Mesophytic – descriptor of plants that prefer moist but well drained soil conditions; such conditions are typically found on lower slopes, in ravines, and in coves.

Nonvascular vegetation – vegetation dominated by lichens, mosses, and liverworts, *i.e.*, biota lacking a structural system of tissue that conducts water and soluble nutrients.

Nutrient-requiring – descriptor of plants that require relatively high levels of soluble nutrients (particularly calcium and magnesium) for successful growth; such species are generally restricted to fertile soils. **Overstory** – the uppermost layer of trees forming the canopy of a forest or woodland.

Shrub – a multi-stemmed woody plant routinely attaining heights between 0.5 and 6 meters.

Tree – a single-stemmed woody plant routinely attaining heights greater than 6 meters.

Understory – collective term for the small trees and shrubs growing beneath the canopy in a forest or woodland.

Wetland indicator – plants indicative of soils subject to seasonal saturation, permanent saturation, or seasonal flooding

Woodland – vegetation dominated by trees at least 6 meters tall producing an open canopy, typically with 5-60% cover; some woodlands may have > 60% canopy cover following elimination or reduction of natural disturbances (*e.g.*, fire).

Xerophytic – descriptor of plants adapted to dry, drought-prone soil environments; such soils are common in the park on areas with abundant exposed or shallow bedrock, and on convex upper slopes and spur ridges, particularly in areas underlain by metasedimentary rocks.

Table 2. List of Indicator Species for Vegetation Classes Used in the Shenandoah National Park Vegetation Field Key.

1 / XEROPHYTIC HERBS	2 / DRY-MESOPHYTIC HERBS	3 / MESOPHYTIC NUTRIENT-REQUIRING HERBS	4 / HIGH-ELEVATION (> 3000 feet elevation) LITHOPHYTIC SPECIES	5 / LOW-ELEVATION (< 2000 feet elevation) LITHOPHYTIC HERBS	6 / WETLAND INDICATOR SPECIES
Aureolaria spp.	*Ageratina altissima*	*Aconitum reclinatum*	*Carex brunnescens*	*Bouteloua curtipendula*	*Alnus incana* ssp. *rugosa*
Carex pensylvanica	*Actaea racemosa*	*Actaea racemosa*	*Carex aestivalis*	*Cheilanthes lanosa*	*Alnus serrulata*
Cunila origanoides	*Amphicarpaea bracteata*	*Agastache scrophulariaefolia*	*Diervilla lonicera*	*Cyperus tupulinus*	*Caltha palustris*
Danthonia spicata	*Asclepias quadrifolia*	*Ageratina altissima*	*Heuchera pubescens*	*Isanthus brachiatus*	*Carex atlantica*
Dichanthelium boscii	*Brachyelytrum erectum*	*Angelica triquinata*	*Huperzia appalachiana*	*Muhlenbergia capillaris*	*Carex bromoides*
Dichanthelium linearifolium	*Circaea lutetiana*	*Arisaema triphyllum*	*Hylotelephium telephioides*	*Oligoneuron rigidum*	*Carex echinata*
Elymus hystrix var. *hystrix*	*Desmodium nudiflorum*	*Asarum canadense*	*Polypodium appalachianum*	*Panicum philadelphicum*	*Carex gynandra*
Eupatorium sessilifolium	*Dichanthelium latifolium*	*Asclepias exaltata*	*Rubus ideaus* ssp. *strigosus*	*Polygonum tenue*	*Carex leptalea*
Helianthus divaricatus	*Dioscorea quaternata*	*Caulophyllum thalictroides*	*Saxifraga michauxii*	*Selaginella rupestris*	*Carex prasina*
Hieracium venosum	*Elymys hystrix* var. *hystrix*	*Collinsonia canadensis*	*Sibbaldiopsis tridentata*	*Sorghastrum nutans*	*Carex scabrata*
Houstonia longifolia	*Eurybia divaricata*	*Deparia acrostichoides*	*Solidago simplex* var. *randii*	*Sporobolus clandestinus*	*Carex stricta*
Ionactis linariifolius	*Eurybia macrophylla*	*Hydrophyllum virginianum*	*Sorbus americana*	*Symphyotrichum oblongifolium*	*Chelone glabra*
Lespedeza procumbens	*Festuca subverticillata*	*Impatiens pallida*		*Talinum teretifolium*	*Chrysosplenium americanum*
Muhlenbergia sobolifera	*Galium circaezans*	*Laportea canadensis*			*Fraxinus nigra*
Potentilla canadensis	*Galium latifolium*	*Monarda clinopodia*			*Glyceria melicaria*
Pteridium aquilinum	*Galium triflorum*	*Osmorhiza claytonii*			*Glyceria striata*
Pycnanthemum incanum	*Hepatica americana*	*Polymnia canadensis*			*Hydrocotyle americana*
Rosa carolina	*Phryma leptostachya*	*Scutellaria serrata*			*Ilex verticillata*
Solidago bicolor	*Polystichum acrostichoides*	*Thalictrum coriaceum*			*Impatiens capensis*
Solidago ulmifolia	*Scrophularia lanceolata*	*Trillium grandiflorum*			*Osmunda cinnamomea*
	Silene stellata	*Viola canadensis*			*Osmunda regalis*
	Solidago caesia				*Oxypolis rigidior*
	Solidago curtisii				*Panicum rigidulum*
	Stellaria pubera				*Panicum verrucosum*
	Uvularia perfoliata				*Platanthera clavellata*
					Quercus palustris
					Sanguisorba canadensis
					Saxifraga micranthidifolia
					Symplocarpus foetidus
					Veratrum viride
					Viola cucullata

1a Modified vegetation with < 50% tree canopy, originating directly from recent disturbance (*e.g.* gypsy moth) or major human landscape alterations (*e.g.*, clearing) ....go to 2
1b Natural and seminatural vegetation with or without a tree canopy, often influenced by past disturbance but largely shaped by natural successional processes and disturbance regimes.........
....go to 3

2a Meadows, lawns, and roadsides dominated by herbaceous vegetation; trees and shrubs may be scattered; low (< 0.5 m tall) patches of *Vaccinium* spp. may be common in some areas; confined to areas around developed facilities, road edges, and the general vicinity of Big Meadows.........
....**Cultural Meadow (M2)**
2b Former forests, with abundant snags and fallen trunks of trees killed by gypsy moth, hemlock adelgid, pine beetle, drought, and/or fire; vegetation commonly of thick shrub and sapling regeneration; widespread in Park ....**Catastrophically Disturbed Forest (M1)**

3a Vegetation of uplands, not influenced by overland flooding or groundwater seepage ....go to 4
3b Vegetation of wetlands, *e.g.*, floodplains, ponds, and groundwater-saturated habitats; surface water or signs of overland flooding (scoured areas, debris piles, etc.) present; at least a few wetland indicator species (Table 1) usually present ....go to 58

4a Trees (> 6 m tall) forming an open to closed canopy; forest and woodland vegetation ...go to 5
4b Tree canopy absent; trees, if present, few and usually < 6 m tall; surficial rock generally abundant; shrub, herbaceous, and nonvascular vegetation of exposed outcrops and talus............
....go to 51

TERRESTRIAL FOREST AND WOODLAND VEGETATION

5a Conifers contributing at least 25% cover to the tree layers (overstory and understory)..............
....go to 6
5b Conifers absent or contributing < 25% cover to the tree layers ....go to 24

FORESTS AND WOODLANDS WITH > 25% CONIFEROUS TREE COVER

6a Stand with variable mixtures of young, even-aged hardwoods and pines, especially *Robinia pseudoacacia*, *Sassafras albidum*, *Fraxinus americana*, *Prunus serotina*, *Crataegus* spp., *Liriodendron tulipifera*, *Acer rubrum*, *Ailanthus altissima*, and *Pinus strobus*, any one of which can dominate over small areas; stand often choked with vines and exotic weeds; old clearings and home sites .... **Northeastern Modified Successional Forest (F21, CEGL006599)**
6b *Robinia pseudoacacia* absent or of very low importance in stand; composition not as above; habitats various ....go to 7

7a Stand on xeric, deeply piled quartzite talus; scrubby woodland dominated by gnarled *Betula lenta*, with or without *Quercus prinus* and *Quercus rubra* (*Pinus* spp. are sometimes important)
.... **Sweet Birch – Chestnut Oak Talus Woodland (F2, CEGL006565)**
7b Stand not on xeric, deeply piled quartzite talus ....go to 8

8a *Juniperus virginiana* with > 25% cover in xeric woodlands with *Fraxinus americana* and *Carya* spp. on and around metabasalt outcrops...

.... **Central Appalachian Basic Woodland (O5, CEGL003683)**
8b *Juniperus virginiana* absent or of low cover in stand ....go to 9

9a *Pinus virginiana* with > 25% cover in stand ....go to 10
9b *Pinus virginiana* absent or of very low cover in stand .... go to 12

10a *Pinus virginiana* dominant in monospecific stands, or co-dominant with young hardwoods in decadent stands; early-successional forests of formerly cleared fields and home sites................
.... **Virginia Pine Successional Forest (F22, CEGL002591)**
10b *Pinus virginiana* mixed with hardwoods in xeric woodlands on and around rock outcrops.....
....go to 11

11a *Pinus virginiana* co-dominant with *Quercus prinus* in xeric woodlands on and around acidic outcrops of various bedrock types ....
....**Central Appalachian Xeric Chestnut Oak – Virginia Pine Woodland (O8, CEGL008540)**
11b *Pinus virginiana* co-dominant with *Fraxinus americana* and *Carya* spp. in xeric woodlands on and around metabasalt outcrops...
....**Central Appalachian Basic Woodland (O5, CEGL003683)**

12a *Tsuga canadensis* strongly dominant, or co-dominant in overstory or understory with *Betula alleghaniensis, Betula lenta, Acer saccharum*, and/or *Quercus rubra*; in sheltered coves and mesic flats at middle to high elevations (2500 to 3300 ft; most common > 3000 ft).................
.... **Hemlock – Northern Hardwood Forest (F8, CEGL006109)**
12b *Tsuga canadensis* not strongly dominant or co-dominant ....go to 13

13a *Betula alleghaniensis* dominant or co-dominant with *Quercus rubra* (*Tsuga canadensis* and/or *Abies balsamea* are sometimes important in stand); usually on steep, rocky, sheltered slopes; at high elevations (> 3000 ft) on metabasalt and granitic substrates only ....
.... **Central Appalachian Northern Hardwood Forest (F7, CEGL008502)**
13b *Betula alleghaniensis* absent or unimportant .... go to 14

14a Mesophytic forests, often with mixed canopy dominance, of stream bottoms, coves, ravines, and concave slopes ....go to 15
14b Drier, oak- and/or pine-dominated forests and woodlands of various, usually more exposed topography ....go to 17

15a Forest with lush herb layer dominated by mesophytic nutrient-demanding herbs (Table 1); *Acer saccharum, Tilia americana, Fraxinus americana* and other hardwoods forming mixed overstories (*Tsuga canadensis* occasionally important in stand) ....
......................................**Central Appalachian Rich Cove Forest (F15, CEGL006237)**
15b Forest with sparse to well-developed herb layer, but not dominated by mesophytic nutrient-demanding herbs (Table 1); variable combinations of *Liriodendron tulipifera, Betula lenta, Tsuga canadensis, Pinus strobus, Acer rubrum, Nyssa sylvatica, Fagus grandifolia*, and/or *Quercus* spp. forming the overstory; bottoms and lower slopes of coves at lower elevations (< 3000 ft) .... go to 16

16a Herb layer patchy to well-developed, with dry-mesophytic herbs (Table 1) prevalent; *Ostrya virginiana* and/or *Lindera benzoin* often present in the understory at low cover; ericaceous

shrubs usually unimportant; *Pinus strobus* and/or *Tsuga canadensis* often important in stand ....
Central Appalachian Acidic Cove Forest (White Pine – Hemlock – Mixed Hardwoods Type) (F12, CEGL006304)

16b Herb layer often poorly developed, or consisting mostly of woody seedlings or fern patches; *Ostrya virginiana* and *Lindera benzoin* usually absent; *Kalmia latifolia* and/or other ericads (*e.g.*, *Menziesia pilosa*, *Rhododendron catawbiense*) usually important in shrub layer; *Pinus strobus* usually absent or unimportant in stand; *Tsuga canadensis* often important, at least in the understory...
Central Appalachian Acidic Cove Forest (Hemlock – Hardwood / Mountain-Laurel Type) (F24, CEGL008512)

17a *Pinus rigida* and/or *Pinus pungens* dominant or co-dominant in stand; forest or woodland.18
17b *Pinus rigida* and *Pinus pungens* absent or minor components of stand; mostly closed-canopy oak forest...go to 19

18a *Pinus rigida* and/or *Pinus pungens* dominant, or co-dominant with *Quercus prinus* and/or *Quercus coccinea*; ericaceous shrubs usually forming dense colonies; *Quercus ilicifolia* often abundant; true herbs absent or sparse; woodland of quartzite and granitic cliff-tops and convex slopes and spur ridges...
.......................**Central Appalachian Pine – Oak / Heath Woodland (F1, CEGL004996)**
18b *Pinus pungens* co-dominant with *Quercus prinus*, *Quercus rubra*, and/or *Pinus virginiana*; ericaceous shrubs sparse to moderately dense; *Quercus ilicifolia* usually absent; xerophytic herbs1 with moderately high cover, the graminoids (*Schizachyrium scoparium*, *Danthonia spicata*, *Carex pensylvanica*, *Deschampsia flexuosa*) most abundant; woodland of sloping and flat acidic outcrops of various... ..
....**Central Appalachian Xeric Chestnut Oak – Virginia Pine Woodland (O8, CEGL008540)**

19a *Quercus rubra* dominant, or co-dominant with *Quercus alba*; *Quercus prinus* absent; on high, upper slopes and crests at 3000 to 4050 ft elevation (*Tsuga canadensis*, *Pinus strobus*, *Abies balsamea*, and/or *Picea rubens* are sometimes important in stand) ....
Northern Red Oak Forest (Pennsylvania Sedge – Wavy Hairgrass Type) (F9, CEGL008506)
19b *Quercus rubra* not solely dominant; *Quercus prinus* present and usually important; occurring below 3000 ft elevation or, if higher, then *Quercus prinus* important in stand ..go to 20

20a *Quercus alba* dominant or co-dominant in stand; hickories important (*Pinus virginiana* and/or *Pinus strobus* are often important); on low-elevation (< 1600 ft) slopes and dry stream terraces .... **Central Appalachian Acidic Oak – Hickory Forest (F18, CEGL008515)**
20b *Quercus alba* not dominant or co-dominant; hickories usually not important; more widely distributed in Park ....go to 21

21a Non-ericaceous species (*e.g.*, *Hamamelis virginiana*, *Acer pensylvanicum*, *Viburnum acerifolium*, *Corylus cornuta*) prevalent in shrub layer; overstory co-dominated by *Quercus prinus* and *Quercus rubra*, with many associated hardwoods (*Pinus strobus* occasionally important) ....
Central Appalachian Dry-Mesic Chestnut Oak – Northern Red Oak Forest (F5,

CEGL006057)

21b Ericaceous species (*e.g.*, *Kalmia latifolia*, *Gaylussacia baccata*, *Vaccinium* spp.) prevalent in shrub and herb layers..go to 22

22a *Quercus prinus* in nearly pure stands, or co-dominant with *Quercus coccinea* and/or *Quercus velutina*; shrub layer dominated by *Kalmia latifolia* or by deciduous ericads (*Pinus* spp. are sometimes important) ....
.... **Central Appalachian / Northern Piedmont Chestnut Oak Forest (F3, CEGL006299)**
22b *Quercus prinus* and *Quercus rubra* co-dominant in stand ....go to 23

23a Deciduous ericads (e.g., *Vaccinium* spp., *Rhododendron periclymenoides*) prevalent in the shrub layer (*Pinus* spp. are sometimes important)...
Central Appalachian Dry Chestnut Oak – Northern Red Oak / Heath Forest (F23, CEGL008523)
23b *Kalmia latifolia* strongly dominant in the shrub layer (*Pinus* spp. are sometimes important) .... **Central Appalachian / Northern Piedmont Chestnut Oak Forest (F3, CEGL006299)**

FORESTS AND WOODLANDS WITH < 25% CONIFEROUS TREE COVER

24a Ericaceous shrubs (*Gaylussacia baccata*, *Kalmia latifolia*, *Lyonia ligustrina*, *Menziesia pilosa*, *Rhododendron* spp., *Vaccinium* spp.) prevalent in the lower woody strata; if sparse, clearly more numerous than non-ericaceous species ....go to 25
24b Ericaceous shrubs absent, or of low to moderate cover and admixed with non-ericaceous genera .... go to 35

DECIDUOUS FORESTS AND WOODLANDS WITH A PREVALENT ERICACEOUS SHRUB COMPONENT

25b *Betula alleghaniensis* dominant or co-dominant in stand; *Acer spicatum* usually important in understory; on rocky, north- to west-facing slopes > 3000 ft elevation ....go to 26
25b *Betula alleghaniensis* absent or unimportant... go to 27

26a *Betula alleghaniensis* dominant or co-dominant with *Quercus rubra* (often with other hardwood associates); stands forming a ~closed forest; usually on, rocky, sheltered slopes with some soil development. **Central Appalachian Northern Hardwood Forest (F7, CEGL008502) 26b** *Betula alleghaniensis* dominant or co-dominant with *Sorbus americana*; *Quercus rubra* absent; *Polypodium appalachianum* and other high-elevation lithophytic species (Table 1) prevalent; stands forming a scrubby, open woodland;, on very steep, deeply piled talus with little or no soil present between boulders
....**Central Appalachian High-Elevation Boulderfield Forest (O4, CEGL008504)**

27a Gnarled, stunted forest or open woodland of *Betula lenta*, with or without *Quercus prinus* and/or *Quercus rubra*, on deeply piled quartzite (occasionally granitic and metabasalt) talus; understory usually limited by rock cover and somewhat to very sparse ....
.... **Sweet Birch – Chestnut Oak Talus Woodland (F2, CEGL006565)**
27b Open to closed-canopy forest of stunted to normal stature, dominated by *Quercus* spp. or

mixed hardwoods, occupying mesic to dry (often rocky) coves, slopes and flats throughout Park; if on talus, then composition not as above ....go to 28

28a On ~ mesic bottoms and lower slopes of coves; stand mixed, with variable combinations of *Liriodendron tulipifera*, *Betula lenta*, *Tsuga canadensis*, *Pinus strobus*, *Acer rubrum*, *Nyssa sylvatica*, *Fagus grandifolia*, and/or *Quercus* spp. forming the overstory...........................
Central Appalachian Acidic Cove Forest (Hemlock – Hardwood / Mountain-Laurel Type) (F24, CEGL008512)
28b On drier slopes, crests, and gentle uplands; stand dominated by *Quercus* spp, with or without *Carya* spp.. ....go to 29

29a *Carya* spp. common or abundant in stand...go to 30
29b *Carya* spp. absent or unimportant in stand...go to 31

30a *Quercus alba* strongly dominant or co-dominant in stand; on low-elevation (< 1600 ft) metasedimentary slopes and dry stream terraces ....
.... **Central Appalachian Acidic Oak – Hickory Forest (F18, CEGL008515)**
30b *Quercus alba* not strongly dominant, occasionally co-dominant; *Quercus prinus* and *Quercus rubra* prevalent in overstory; on metasedimentary ridges at middle elevations (2200 to 3350 ft) ....
... **Central Appalachian Montane Oak – Hickory Forest (Acidic Type) (F17, CEGL008516)**

31a *Quercus rubra* dominant, or co-dominant with *Quercus alba*; *Quercus prinus* absent; on high, upper slopes and crests at 3000 to 4050 ft elevation ....
Northern Red Oak Forest (Pennsylvania Sedge – Wavy Hairgrass Type) (F9, CEGL008506)
31b *Quercus rubra* not solely dominant; *Quercus prinus* present and usually important; occurring below 3000 ft elevation or, if higher, then *Quercus prinus* important in stand ..go to 32

32a *Quercus alba* important in mixed stands with *Quercus coccinea*, *Quercus velutina*, and *Quercus prinus*; on gentle slopes and flats at the lowest elevations (< 1900 ft); ericaceous shrubs mostly deciduous .... **Low-Elevation Mixed Oak / Heath Forest (F4, CEGL008521)**
32b *Quercus alba* absent or unimportant; more widespread and at higher elevations; ericaceous shrubs mostly deciduous, mostly evergreen, or mixed ....go to 33

33a *Quercus prinus* in nearly pure stands, or co-dominant with *Quercus coccinea* and/or *Quercus velutina*; shrub layer dominated by *Kalmia latifolia* or by deciduous ericads ....
.... **Central Appalachian / Northern Piedmont Chestnut Oak Forest (F3, CEGL006299)**
33b *Quercus prinus* and *Quercus rubra* co-dominant in stand ....go to 34

34a Deciduous ericads (e.g., *Vaccinium* spp., *Rhododendron periclymenoides*) prevalent in the shrub layer; *Kalmia latifolia*, if present, clearly less abundant than the deciduous ericads ....
Central Appalachian Dry Chestnut Oak – Northern Red Oak / Heath Forest (F23, CEGL008523)
34b *Kalmia latifolia* strongly dominant in the shrub layer, either > 50% cover or clearly more abundant than deciduous ericads in aggregate ....
..........**Central Appalachian / Northern Piedmont Chestnut Oak Forest (F3, CEGL006299)**

DECIDUOUS FORESTS AND WOODLANDS LACKING A PREVALENT ERICACEOUS SHRUB COMPONENT

35a *Betula alleghaniensis* dominant or co-dominant in stand; *Acer spicatum* usually important in understory; on rocky, north- to west-facing slopes > 3000 ft elevation ....go to 36
35b *Betula alleghaniensis* absent or unimportant ....go to 37

36a *Betula alleghaniensis* dominant or co-dominant with *Quercus rubra* (often with other hardwood associates); stands forming a ~closed forest; usually on, rocky, sheltered slopes with some soil development **Central Appalachian Northern Hardwood Forest (F7, CEGL008502)**
36b *Betula alleghaniensis* dominant or co-dominant with *Sorbus americana*; *Quercus rubra* absent; *Polypodium appalachianum* and other high-elevation lithophytic species (Table 1) prevalent; stands forming a scrubby, open woodland;, on very steep, deeply piled talus with little or no soil present between boulders...
.............................Central Appalachian High-Elevation Boulderfield Forest (O4, CEGL008504)

37a Gnarled, stunted forest or open woodland of *Betula lenta*, with or without *Quercus prinus* and/or *Quercus rubra*, on deeply piled quartzite (occasionally granitic and metabasalt) talus; understory usually limited by rock cover and somewhat to very sparse ....
.... **Sweet Birch – Chestnut Oak Talus Woodland (F2, CEGL006565)**
37b Open to closed-canopy forest of stunted to normal stature, dominated by *Quercus* spp. or mixed hardwoods, occupying mesic to dry (often rocky) coves, slopes and flats throughout Park; if on talus, then composition not as above ....go to 38

38a Stand with variable mixtures of young, even-aged hardwoods and pines, especially *Robinia pseudoacacia*, *Sassafras albidum*, *Fraxinus americana*, *Prunus serotina*, *Crataegus* spp., *Liriodendron tulipifera*, *Acer rubrum*, *Ailanthus altissima*, and *Pinus strobus*, any one of which can dominate over small areas; stand often choked with vines and exotic weeds; old clearings and home sites .... **Northeastern Modified Successional Forest (F21, CEGL006599)**
38b *Robinia pseudoacacia* absent or of very low importance in stand; composition not as above; habitats various ....go to 39

39a *Liriodendron tulipifera* dominant in a monospecific, even-aged stand; herb layer often weedy and dominated by exotic species (*e.g.*, *Alliaria petiolata*, *Polygonum cespitosum*); early-successional forest of formerly cleared coves, ravines, and fertile slopes, mostly below 2600 ft elevation .... **Successional Tuliptree Forest (Circumneutral Type) (F13, CEGL007220)**
39b Overstory more mixed and/or uneven-aged; later-successional forest; habitats various ....
....go to 40

40a Forest with lush herb layer dominated by mesophytic nutrient-demanding herbs (Table 1)
....go to 41
40b Forest with sparse to well-developed herb layer, but not dominated by mesophytic nutrient-demanding herbs (Table 1) ....go to 44

41a Forest (sometimes very open) on deeply piled metabasalt or granitic talus with ample interstitial soil development; surface cover of boulders and stones usually > 50%; overstory

92

dominated by *Fraxinus americana* and/or *Tilia americana*, often with *Quercus rubra*, *Carya* spp. and *Betula lenta*; *Ostrya virginiana* and/or *Acer pensylvanicum* important in understory; scrambling lianas (*Parthenocissus quinquefolia*, *Toxicodendron radicans*, *Vitis* spp.) often abundant; mesophytic nutrient-demanding herbs (Table 1) characteristic but often somewhat limited by the rock substrate ....
...................................**Central Appalachian Basic Boulderfield Forest (F14, CEGL008528)**
41b Forests of various habitats, often rocky but not of deeply piled talus; surface cover of loose rocks usually < 50%; woody composition not as above; cover of mesophytic nutrient-demanding herbs (Table 1) usually more continuous ....go to 42

42a Forest of middle to upper slopes and gentle crests, mostly above 2500 ft elevation; *Quercus rubra* dominant, or co-dominant with *Quercus alba*, *Carya* spp., and/or *Fraxinus americana*.......
...... **Central Appalachian Montane Oak – Hickory Forest (Basic Type) (F16, CEGL008518)**
42b Forest of middle to lower, often concave slopes, ravines, and coves; mesophytic trees (*e.g.*, *Liriodendron tulipifera*, *Tilia americana*, *Acer saccharum*, *Fraxinus americana*) dominant .....
....go to 43

43a *Acer saccharum* important in the overstory, or abundant in the understory ....
.... **Central Appalachian Rich Cove Forest (F15, CEGL006237)**
43b *Acer saccharum* absent, or sparse in understory only...
.... **Southern Appalachian Cove Forest (Typic Type) (F10, CEGL007710)**

44a On mesic bottoms and lower slopes of coves; variable combinations of *Liriodendron tulipifera*, *Betula lenta*, *Tsuga canadensis*, *Pinus strobus*, *Acer rubrum*, *Nyssa sylvatica*, *Fagus grandifolia*, and/or *Quercus* spp. forming the overstory ....go to 45
44b On drier slopes and crests; overstory dominated by *Quercus* spp., *Carya* spp., and/or *Fraxinus americana* .... go to 46

45a Herb layer patchy to well-developed, with dry-mesophytic herbs (Table 1) prevalent; *Ostrya virginiana* and/or *Lindera benzoin* often present in the understory at low cover; *Pinus strobus* and/or *Tsuga canadensis* often present at low cover..
Central Appalachian Acidic Cove Forest (White Pine – Hemlock – Mixed Hardwoods Type) (F12, CEGL006304)
45b Herb layer often poorly developed, or consisting mostly of woody seedlings or fern patches; *Ostrya virginiana* and *Lindera benzoin* usually absent; *Pinus strobus* usually absent or unimportant in stand; *Tsuga canadensis* usually present at low cover ....
Central Appalachian Acidic Cove Forest (Hemlock – Hardwood / Mountain-Laurel Type) (F24, CEGL008512)

46a Canopy partially to very open and trees stunted; *Fraxinus americana* and/or *Carya* spp. usually co-dominant; *Quercus* spp. absent or unimportant; xerophytic (Table 1) and low-elevation lithophytic herbs (Table 1) prevalent; woodlands of steep, very rocky slopes with numerous metabasalt outcrops ...... **Central Appalachian Basic Woodland (O5, CEGL003683)**
46b Canopy essentially closed (excepting temporary wind or gypsy-moth disturbances), with trees of normal stature; *Quercus* spp. prevalent, often co-dominant with *Carya* spp.; *Fraxinus americana* a characteristic but minor overstory associate; xerophytic (Table 1) and/or dry-

mesophytic (Table 1) herbs prevalent; forests of various topographic and geologic settings………
………………………………………………………………………………………………………go to 47

47a *Quercus rubra* dominant, or co-dominant with *Quercus alba*; *Quercus prinus* absent; on high, upper slopes and crests at 3000 to 4050 ft elevation………………………………………
Northern Red Oak Forest (Pennsylvania Sedge – Wavy Hairgrass Type) (F9, CEGL008506)
47b *Quercus rubra* not solely dominant; *Quercus prinus* present and usually important; occurring below 3000 ft elevation or, if higher, then *Quercus prinus* important in stand ..go to 48

48a *Quercus alba* strongly dominant or co-dominant in stand with other oaks and hickories; *Pinus strobus* and/or *Pinus virginiana* often present in the overstory; on low-elevation (< 1600 ft) metasedimentary slopes and dry stream terraces …………………………………………
……………………..**Central Appalachian Acidic Oak – Hickory Forest (F18, CEGL008515)**
48b *Quercus alba* not strongly dominant, occasionally co-dominant; *Quercus prinus* and *Quercus rubra* prevalent in overstory; *Pinus strobus* and/or *Pinus virginiana* absent or unimportant; more widespread and/or at higher elevations ……………………………go to 49

49a Mixed oak forest (*Carya* spp. usually unimportant); *Betula lenta*, *Acer pensylvanicum*, and/or *Hamamelis virginiana* usually important; often on talus…………………………………
Central Appalachian Dry-Mesic Chestnut Oak – Northern Red Oak Forest (F5, CEGL006057)
49b Oak-hickory forest (*Carya* spp. usually abundant); *Betula lenta*, *Acer pensylvanicum*, and *Hamamelis virginiana* usually unimportant; rarely on talus ……………………………go to 50

50a Forest of phyllite/metasandstone substrates on metasedimentary ridges at middle elevations (2250 to 3350 ft) …… …………………………………………………………………………
…**Central Appalachian Montane Oak – Hickory Forest (Acidic Type) (F17, CEGL008516)**
50b Forest of metabasalt and granitic substrates on slopes at low and middle elevations (1200 to 2800 ft) …………………………………………………………………………………………
Central Appalachian Basic Oak – Hickory Forest (Submontane/Foothills Type) (F19, CEGL008514)

VEGETATION OF ROCK OUTCROPS AND NONVASCULAR BOULDERFIELDS

51a Substrate of deeply piled boulder and stone talus; vascular plants absent over patches of at least 100 m^2 …………………………………………………………………………go to 52
51b Exposed bedrock prevalent, stones and large boulders may also be present; vascular plants present (sometimes sparse) ……………………………………………………………………go to 53

52a Lichen-dominated boulderfields of Chilhowee Group quartzite …………………………………
……………………………..... **Central Appalachian Acidic Boulderfield (O9, CEGL004142)**
52b Lichen-dominated boulderfields of Catoctin metabasalt ……………………….……………....
………………………..………**Central Appalachian Mafic Boulderfield (O10, CEGL004143)**

53a Stunted *Pinus rigida* and/or *Pinus pungens* present and characteristic among ericaceous shrubs; herbs absent or very sparse; exposed metasedimentary and granitic clifftops and massive

outcrops; lithophytic variants of...
Central Appalachian Pine – Oak / Heath Woodland (F1, CEGL004996)

53b *Pinus rigida* and *Pinus pungens* absent or very sparse ....go to 54

54a Stunted *Fraxinus americana* present and characteristic; high-elevation lithophytic species4
(except *Hylotelephium telephioides*) absent ....go to 55
54b *Fraxinus americana* absent; high-elevation lithophytic species4 present
...............................56

55a Patchy herbaceous and scrub vegetation of low-elevation (1400 to 2400 ft) metabasalt
outcrops; *Juniperus virginiana*, *Cercis canadensis*, *Rhus aromatica*, and/or *Cheilanthes lanosa*
usually present and characteristic; low-elevation lithophytic herbs5 important; *Physocarpus
opulifolius* and *Rhus typhina* not abundant, usually absent; *Symphyotrichum laeve* var.
concinnum and *Hylotelephium telephioides* usually absent ....
...............................**Central Appalachian Circumneutral Barren (O7, CEGL006037)**

55b Patchy herbaceous and scrub vegetation of middle-elevation (1800 to 3450 ft) metabasalt
and granitic outcrops; *Juniperus virginiana*, *Cercis canadensis*, *Rhus aromatica*, and/or
Cheilanthes lanosa absent; low-elevation lithophytic herbs5 mostly absent; *Physocarpus
opulifolius* and/or *Rhus typhina* often abundant; *Symphyotrichum laeve* var. *concinnum* and
Hylotelephium telephioides present and characteristic ....
...............................**Central Appalachian Mafic Barren (O6, CEGL008529)**

56a Shrubland of high-elevation (> 3000 ft) granitic outcrops; *Kalmia latifolia* generally
dominant; herbaceous patches absent or sparse ....
...............................**Central Appalachian Heath Barren (O2, CEGL003939)**
56b Shrubland or patchy herbaceous / scrub vegetation of high-elevation (> 2850 ft) metabasalt
outcrops; *Kalmia latifolia* often present but not dominant ....go to 57

57a *Photinia melanocarpa* and *Gaylussacia baccata* characteristic and dominant (singly or
together) in dense, low shrub patches among the rocks; herbaceous patches usually sparse or
limited ....
**High-Elevation Outcrop Barren (Black Chokeberry Igneous / Metamorphic Type) (O3,
CEGL008508)**
57b *Photinia melanocarpa* and *Gaylussacia baccata* often present, but not particularly
characteristic and intermixed with tree saplings and non-ericaceous species (e.g., *Diervilla
lonicera*, *Physocarpus opulifolius*); herbaceous patches usually well developed (except in
heavily trampled sites), with *Deschampsia flexuosa*, *Solidago simplex* var. *randii*, *Hylotelephium
telephioides*, and/or *Sibbaldiopsis tridentata* often locally abundant ....
...............................**High-Elevation Greenstone Barren (O1, CEGL008536)**

WETLAND VEGETATION

58a Forested wetlands ....go to 59
58b Wetlands lacking a forest canopy ....go to 66

FORESTED WETLANDS

59a Forests of alluvial floodplains and stream bottoms; signs of overland flooding (scoured areas, debris piles, etc.) usually present; wetland indicator species (Table 1) usually sparse or even absent ....go to 60

59b Forests of other wetland habitats; wetland indicator species (Table 1) usually more numerous ....go to 62

60a Low-elevation floodplains filled with bouldery quartzite alluvium; habitats often dry and wetland indicator species (Table 1) absent; forest vegetation characterized by *Quercus alba*, *Pinus strobus*, other *Quercus* spp. and *Carya* spp.; valley-bottom variant of ....
.........................**Central Appalachian Acidic Oak – Hickory Forest (F18, CEGL008515)**
60b Floodplains with alluvium derived from various bedrock types (metabasalt, granitic, metasedimentary); habitats mesic, supporting mesophytic forest vegetation and at least a few wetland indicator species Table 1); oaks absent or occurring in admixture with mesophytic tree species...go to 61

61a *Platanus occidentalis* usually present in mixture with a wide variety of other tree species; *Ulmus americana*, *Juglans nigra*, *Fraxinus pennsylvanica*, and/or *Carpinus caroliniana* often present (may be at low cover); *Betula alleghaniensis* absent or of very low importance; diverse forests of well-developed floodplains at the lowest elevations (< 2000 ft)............................
.... **Northern Blue Ridge Montane Alluvial Forest (F11, CEGL006255)**
61b Low-elevation floodplain species (*Platanus occidentalis*, *Ulmus americana*, *Juglans nigra*, *Fraxinus pennsylvanica*, and *Carpinus caroliniana*) absent; *Betula alleghaniensis* abundant; less diverse forests of montane stream bottoms at middle elevations (> 2000 ft) ....
.... **Hemlock – Northern Hardwood Forest (F8, CEGL006109)**

62a Vegetation of discrete basin wetlands with seasonal ponding; *Panicum rigidulum* and *Panicum verrucosum* characteristic of late-season herbaceous flora in draw-down zones; *Quercus palustris* may form a sparse or open canopy; confined to low-elevation flats where the Park intersects the Shenandoah Valley...
.........................**Shenandoah Valley Sinkhole Pond (Typic Type) (W6, CEGL007858)****
62b Vegetation not associated with a discrete basin; hydrologic regime of groundwater seepage rather than seasonal flooding; *Panicum* spp. and *Quercus palustris* absent ....go to 63

63a Very narrow, linear-patch seepage wetland within forested upland; trees absent (although habitat is shaded by adjacent upland trees) or *Betula alleghaniensis* the only tree rooted in the seep .... **Central Appalachian Woodland Seep (W3, CEGL006258)****
63b Larger forested swamps with water-tolerant trees and shrubs rooted in the seep ....go to 64

64a *Tsuga canadensis* and *Fraxinus* spp. absent; *Nyssa sylvatica* abundant; *Vaccinium corymbosum* and/or *Vaccinium fuscatum* present and characteristic; sphagnous swamps on metasedimentary substrates at very low elevations (< 1800 ft) ....
..............................**Central Appalachian Acidic Seepage Swamp (W2, CEGL007853)****
64b *Tsuga canadensis* and/or *Fraxinus* spp. often common or abundant; *Nyssa sylvatica* usually

absent; *Vaccinium corymbosum* and *Vaccinium fuscatum* absent; swamps on metabasalt and granitic substrates at low to middle elevations (1400 to 3400 ft) ....go to 65

65a *Tsuga canadensis* absent or present; *Fraxinus nigra* often important in the overstory and/or understory; *Pinus strobus*, *Kalmia latifolia* and *Ilex montana* generally absent; *Carex bromoides*, *Carex prasina*, *Deparia acrostichoides*, and *Glyceria striata* usually present and characteristic; *Osmunda cinnamomea* and *Glyceria melicaria* not abundant ....
...............................**Central Appalachian Basic Seepage Swamp (W4, CEGL008416)****
65b *Tsuga canadensis* often characteristic in overstory (formerly abundant prior to adelgid outbreaks); *Fraxinus nigra* absent or unimportant; *Pinus strobus*, *Kalmia latifolia* and *Ilex montana* often present; *Carex bromoides*, *Carex prasina*, *Deparia acrostichoides*, and *Glyceria striata* absent or unimportant; *Osmunda cinnamomea* and *Glyceria melicaria* usually abundant
.... **High-Elevation Hemlock – Yellow Birch Seepage Swamp (W5, CEGL008533)****

NON-FORESTED WETLANDS

66a Herbaceous vegetation of discrete basin wetlands with seasonal ponding; *Panicum rigidulum* and *Panicum verrucosum* characteristic of late-season herbaceous flora in draw-down zones; *Quercus palustris* and/or shrubs may occur on the periphery; confined to low-elevation flats where the Park intersects the Shenandoah Valley...
.........................**Shenandoah Valley Sinkhole Pond (Typic Type) (W6, CEGL007858)****
66b Vegetation not associated with a discrete basin; hydrologic regime of groundwater seepage rather than seasonal flooding; *Panicum* spp. and *Quercus palustris* absent ....go to 67

67a Shrubs, if present, characterized by *Lindera benzoin*; forbs such as *Chelone glabra*, *Chrysosplenium americanum*, and *Caltha palustris* characteristic of the herb layer; graminoids absent or sparse; very narrow, linear-patch seepage wetland within forested upland; widespread in Park .... **Central Appalachian Woodland Seep (W3, CEGL006258)****
67b Shrub layer patchy to well-developed, characterized by *Cornus racemosa*, *Spiraea alba* var. *latifolia*, *Betula populifolia*, and/or *Lyonia ligustrina*; *Lindera benzoin* absent; herb layer characterized by the forb *Sanguisorba canadensis* and large graminoid patches of *Calamagrostis canadensis*, *Carex scoparia*, *Carex bromoides*, *Carex buxbaumii*, and *Glycera striata*; *Chelone glabra* and *Chrysosplenium americanum* absent; confined to high-elevation streamheads over metabasalt in the vicinity of Big Meadow ....
....**Northern Blue Ridge Mafic Fen (W1, CEGL006249)**

** These wetland communities typically occur in very small, often linear patches below minimum mapping unit sizes, and are not mapped in ver. 2.0 of the Shenandoah National Park vegetation map. They may, however, be encountered as inclusions within various upland forest types.

EXHIBIT 6: FIELD KEY TO THE VEGETATION TYPES OF JOSHUA TREE NATIONAL PARK (adapted from Keeler-Wolf et al. 2005)

HOW TO USE THE KEY:

This is not a dichotomous key; there are often more than two choices for each section. Read all options in each list to choose the best match for your vegetation stand. The key will direct you first to the life forms: tree, shrub, and herbaceous, then lead you through more specific lists based on dominant/characteristic or presence/absence of significant species.

Due to the high diversity of the vegetation communities in the area, this is a complex key. You will need to collect plant composition data that includes not only those species that are dominant but also those "indicator," or characteristic species, whose presence may cause the plot to key to another vegetation type.

If there is a species present in high cover for which no type exists in the key, there are two options. First, the plot can key to another species that is present in high cover. For example, a plot with 35 percent cover toyon and 30 percent holly-leaved cherry would key to holly-leaved cherry, since there is no toyon type defined in the study area. If this is not a reasonable option, the plot can be designated "unable to key." Plots that are unable to key may be candidates for new vegetation types.

Estimating cover using actual percentages, rather than cover classes, is preferable, because it gives the fullest picture of the vegetation present. It enables later review of the data to confirm choice of plant community and may help to describe new vegetation types and answer future management or research questions. If a less rigorous and faster approach is needed, for example, if the project is not primarily a vegetation project, the following cover classes are compatible with the key and may be used:

1. <1 percent
2. 1–5 percent
3a. 6–15 percent
3b. 16–25 percent
4. 26–50 percent
5. 51–75 percent
6. 76–100 percent

Using percent Cover Data to Arrive at a Plant Vegetation Type

All references to percent cover in the key are to absolute cover unless specified in a particular section as relative cover.

Absolute cover: The actual percentage of the surface area of the plot that is covered by a species or physiognomic group (trees, shrubs, herbaceous), as in "creosote bush covers 10 percent of the plot." Absolute cover of all species or physiognomic groups, when added together, may total greater than 100 percent, because this is not a proportional number and plants can overlap each other. For example, a plot could have 25 percent tree cover, 40 percent shrub cover, and 50 percent herbaceous cover.

Relative cover: The percentage of the surface area of the plot that is covered by one species or physiognomic group (trees, shrubs, herbaceous) as compared or relative to the amount of surface of the plot covered by all species or groups. Thus, 50 percent relative cover means that half of the total proportion of cover of all species or physiognomic groups is composed of the single species or group in question. Relative cover values are a proportional number that, when added together, total 100 percent for each plot. For example, a Creosote bush–burro bush vegetation plot with 5 percent cover creosote bush and 5 percent cover burro bush estimated using absolute cover would translate to 50 percent relative cover of creosote bush and 50 percent relative cover of burro bush.

TERMS AND CONCEPTS USED THROUGHOUT THE KEY:

DOMINANCE

Dominance by layer: Tree, shrub, and herbaceous layers are considered physiognomically distinct. A vegetation type is considered to belong to a certain physiognomic group if it is dominated by one layer. Layers are prioritized in order of height. The tallest layer, if it meets a criterion in the "characterized" definitions (see below) is said to dominate, and the type is usually named at the Alliance level by the characteristic species of the tallest layer.

Dominant: >50 percent relative cover. Dominance refers to the preponderance of vegetation cover in a stand of uniform composition and site history. It may refer to cover of an individual species (as in "dominated by Douglas-fir", or it may refer to dominance by a physiognomic group, as in "dominated by shrubs." Dominance refers to the relative cover of one species or physiognomic group as compared to another species or physiognomic group. Anything more than 50 percent relative cover is said to dominate a stand, however, see "dominance by layer", below.

Strongly dominant: 60 percent+ relative cover. A species in the dominant life form has 60 percent or greater relative cover.

Codominant: Each species has 30 percent–60 percent relative cover. Codominance refers to two or more species in a stand with near equal cover . In general, codominance can occur among species that have between 30 and 60 percent relative cover each.

Significant: 1 percent–5 percent absolute cover. A species has 1 to 5 percent absolute cover.

Important: >1 percent absolute cover. A species is considered important if it has greater than 1 percent absolute cover. This term is contrasted with dominant to mean that the species is always present in greater than 1 percent cover but not always dominant.

STAND PHYSIOGNOMY

Tree-characterized vegetation: Trees are evenly distributed throughout the stand, with typically ≥10 percent cover, providing a consistent (even if sparse) structural component, and one or both of the following criteria are met: (1) Trees influence the distribution or population dynamics of other plant species; (2) Trees play an important role in ecological processes within the stand.

Shrub-characterized vegetation: Shrubs (including dwarf-shrubs) are evenly distributed throughout the stand, providing a consistent (even if sparse) structural component, and one or both of the following criteria are met: (1) Shrubs influence the distribution or population dynamics of other plant species; (2) Shrubs play an important role in ecological processes within the stand.

Herb-characterized vegetation: Herbs are evenly distributed throughout the stand, providing a consistent (even if sparse) structural component, and play an important role in ecological processes within the stand.

Nonvascular vegetation: Nonvascular organisms provide a consistent (even if sparse) structural component and play an important role in ecological processes within the stand.

OTHER IMPORTANT TERMS

Alliance: Plant communities based on dominant/diagnostic species of uppermost or dominant stratum. Part of the USNVC hierarchy.

Association: The most botanically detailed plant community designation based on dominant species and multiple co- or subdominant indicator species from any strata. Part of the USNVC system.

Diagnostic species: A species typically found in the dominant stratum of a vegetation Association and lending its name to that Association.

Shrub: A multistemmed plant with noticeably woody stems that is between 0.2 and 5 meters tall.

Subshrub: A multistemmed plant with noticeably woody stems less than 0.5 meters tall.

Plant community nomenclature: Species separated by "-" are within the same stratum; species separated by "/" are in different strata. The number at the end of some plant community names is the Mapping Code used for labeling plant community polygons for the associated GIS-based plant community map.

Stand: The basic physical unit of plant communities in a landscape. It has no set size. Some vegetation stands are very small, such as certain wetland types, and some may be several square kilometers in size, such as certain forest types. A stand is defined by two main unifying characteristics:

1. It has compositional integrity. Throughout the stand, the combination of species is similar. The stand is differentiated from adjacent stands by a discernible boundary that may be abrupt or occur indistinctly along an ecological gradient.

2. It has structural integrity. It has a similar history or environmental setting that affords relatively similar horizontal and vertical spacing of plant species. For example, a hillside forest originally dominated by the same species that burned on the upper part of the slopes but not the lower would be divided into two stands. Likewise, a sparse woodland occupying a slope with very shallow rocky soils would be considered a different stand from an adjacent slope with deeper, moister soil and a denser woodland or forest of the same species.

The structural and compositional features of a stand are often combined into a term called homogeneity. For an area of vegetated ground to meet the requirements of a stand, it must be homogeneous at the scale being considered. The associated plant community mapping project had a Minimum Mapping Unit (MMU) of 0.5 hectares.

KEY TO MAJOR VEGETATION DIVISIONS:

I. Vegetation characterized by trees (at least 3 m tall). Trees are evenly distributed throughout the stand but may form a sparse cover over denser subcanopies of shrub and herbaceous species.

Division T: Tree Vegetation

II. Vegetation dominated by shrubs or subshrubs. Trees, if present, are rare and not evenly distributed across the stand and generally form less than 1 percent cover.

Division S: Shrub Vegetation

III. Vegetation characterized by herbaceous species including grasses, grass-like plants, and broad-leaved, herbaceous species.

Division H: Herbaceous Vegetation

Division T: Tree Vegetation

Tree species are present. Trees are defined as woody perennials that are regularly over 3 m in height including shrub species often taller than 3 m such as *Chilopsis linearis*, *Prosopis glandulosa*, *Tamarix* spp. and *Juniperus californica*. The tree layer is visibly uniform in the stand, although it may be low in cover.

Three sections are included: (1) coniferous trees, (2) broadleaf evergreen and deciduous trees, and (3) microphyllous trees.

Section T.I

T.I. Stands characterized by coniferous evergreen trees including *Pinus monophylla* and *Juniperus californica*.
Needle-Leaved Evergreen Woodland

T.I.A. *Pinus monophylla* >=1 percent and generally less than 25 percent cover. *Juniperus californica* may be present. *Pinus monophylla* occurs over a sparse to relatively dense cover of shrubs. Restricted to cool, relatively moist sites of the upper elevations mostly in Little San Bernardino Mountains, but isolated stands in Coxcomb Mountains.
Single-Leaf Pinyon *(Pinus monophylla)* Wooded Shrubland Alliance

Two Associations have been described from JOTR.

> **T.I.A.1.** The scattered tree layer is dominated by *Pinus monophylla* with *Quercus cornelius-mulleri* as dominant in the shrub layer, respectively.
> **Singleleaf Pinyon Pine/Muller's Oak *(Pinus monophylla/Quercus cornelius-mulleri)* Woodland Association**

> **T.I.A.2.** The scattered tree layer has *Juniperus californica* mixed with *Pinus monophylla* and does not have a regular presence of the shrub *Quercus cornelius-mulleri*. Desert Needlegrass (*Achnatherum speciosum*) is characteristic of the understory.
> **Singleleaf Pinyon Pine/California Juniper/Desert Needlegrass *(Pinus monophylla/Juniperus californica/Achnatherum speciosum)* Woodland Association**

T.I.B. The short tree (or large shrub) layer is characterized by California Juniper (*Juniperus californica*) with no other tree species equaling or exceeding cover of *J. californica*, though other species (*Pinus monophylla, Yucca brevifolia*) may be present in small amounts (usually <1 percent cover).
California Juniper *(Juniperus californica)* Woodland Alliance

This Alliance is represented by five different Associations in JOTR.

> **T.I.B.1.** *J. californica* is the characteristic short tree or tall shrub, mixing with the scrub oak *Quercus cornelius-mulleri*. The small shrub *Coleogyne ramosissima* is characteristic in the understory.
> **California Juniper - Muller Oak - Blackbush *(Juniperus californica - Quercus cornelius-mulleri/Coleogyne ramosissima)* Woodland Association**

> **T.I.B.2.** *J. californica* occurs as a tall shrub or low tree with the shrubby Mojave Yucca, and the short shrub *Coleogyne ramosissima* is characteristic in the understory.
> **California Juniper /Blackbush - Mojave Yucca *(Juniperus californica/Coleogyne ramosissima - Yucca schidigera)* Woodland Association**

T.I.B.3. *J. californica* occurs with *Yucca schidigera. Coleogyne* is absent or very low cover and the medium tall bunch grass *Pleuraphis rigida* is characteristic of the understory
California Juniper - Mojave Yucca/Big Galleta *(Juniperus californica - (Yucca schidigera)/Pleuraphis rigida)* Woodland Association

T.I.B.4. *J. californica* is the principal tall shrub or small tree over a relatively simple understory characterized by the low shrub *Coleogyne ramosissima.*
California Juniper/Blackbush *(Juniperus californica/Coleogyne ramosissima)* Woodland Association

T.I.B.5. *J. californica* is the characteristic small tree or large shrub with a mixture of other shrub species including the characteristic yucca-like *Nolina parryi.*
California Juniper/Beargrass *(Juniperus californica/Nolina parryi)* Woodland Association

Section T.II

T.II. Stands characterized by nonconiferous trees including broad-leaf evergreen or deciduous species.
Broad-Leaved Woodland and Forest

T.II.A. Stands characterized by tall monocot trees of Southwest Desert affinities.

T.II.A.1. Stands characterized by the California Fan Palm (*Washingtonia filifera*), associated with springs and moist canyon bottoms in a few places in the park. Other riparian tree species (*Populus fremontii, Salix laevigata*) may be associated with them and may be codominant.
California Fan Palm (*Washingtonia filifera*) Alliance

T.II.A.2. Stands characterized by the Joshua Tree (*Yucca brevifolia*). *Y. brevifolia* maintains at least 1 percent cover, evenly distributed across the stand. Dominant understory species are shrub species such as *Coleogyne ramosissima, Opuntia ramosissima,* or the perennial grass *Pleuraphis rigida.* Common in shallow, upland soils throughout the mid and upper elevations of the park. *Yucca brevifolia* and *Juniperus californica* may both codominate in the tree or tall shrub layer. If *Pinus monophylla* and *Yucca brevifolia* codominate, then use *Pinus monophylla* Alliance.
Joshua Tree *(Yucca brevifolia)* Wooded Shrubland Alliance

Six Associations have been tentatively defined from the park.

T.II.A.2.a. *Yucca brevifolia* forms a widely scattered emergent but evenly distributed overstory over the more abundant short shrub *Coleogyne ramosissima.*
Joshua Tree/Blackbush *(Yucca brevifolia/Coleogyne ramosissima)* Wooded Shrubland Association

T.II.A.2.b. *Yucca brevifolia* and *Juniperus californica* codominate (usually between 1 percent and 5 percent cover each) in the tall shrub or tree layer with *Coleogyne ramosissima* as the principle understory shrub.
Joshua Tree/California Juniper/Blackbush *(Yucca brevifolia/Juniperus californica/Coleogyne ramosissima)* Wooded Shrubland Association

T.II.A.2.c. *Yucca brevifolia* and *Juniperus californica* both codominate between 1 percent and 5 percent cover, with Nevada Ephedra as the principal understory shrub.
Joshua Tree/California Juniper/Nevada Ephedra *(Yucca brevifolia - Juniperus californica/Ephedra nevadensis)* Wooded Shrubland Association

T.II.A.2.d. *Yucca brevifolia* occurs in upper bajada washes and arroyo margins with the large rosaceous shrub *Prunus fasciculata* as the principal understory species.
Joshua Tree/Desert Almond *(Yucca brevifolia/Prunus fasciculata)* Wooded Shrubland Association

T.II.A.2.e. *Yucca brevifolia* occurs as a regularly distributed emergent over a shrub understory of Creosote Bush and Mojave Yucca. These stands typically occur on lower elevation slopes and alluvial fans than the previously listed Associations.
Joshua Tree/Creosote Bush – Mojave Yucca *(Yucca brevifolia/Larrea tridentata - Yucca schidigera)* Wooded Shrubland Association

T.II.A.2.f. *Yucca brevifolia* occurs as a regularly distributed emergent over Creosote Bush with the bunchgrass *Pleuraphis rigida* common and evenly distributed in the understory.
Joshua Tree/Creosote Bush/Big Galleta *(Yucca brevifolia/Larrea tridentata - Pleuraphis rigida)* Wooded Shrubland Association

T.II.B. Stands characterized by widespread winter-deciduous, broad-leaved (including pinnate-leaved, e.g., *Prosopis*) species of trees or tall shrubs usually associated with places that remain moist throughout the growing season.

T.II.B.1. The spreading tall shrub or short tree, Honey Mesquite (*Prosopis glandulosa*), is dominant (at least 2 percent absolute cover). If other tree or large shrub species are present, none have more cover or are any taller. Associated with alkaline wetlands and dune margins locally in the eastern portion of the park.
Honey Mesquite (*Prosopis glandulosa*) Woodland Alliance (no Associations defined for the park)

T.II.B.2. The broad-leaved deciduous tree Fremont Cottonwood (*Populus Fremontii)* is conspicuous and the dominant tree throughout the stand. Associated with springs scattered throughout the park, may be mixed with Willow (Salix) species at lower cover.

Fremont Cottonwood (*Populus fremontii*) Woodland Alliance (no Associations defined for this project)

T.II.B.3. Red Willow (*Salix laevigata*) is the dominant tree in stands, usually associated with permanent moisture in canyons and at springs, occasional throughout the park.
Red Willow (*Salix laevigata*) Forest Alliance (no Associations defined for the park)

Section T.III

T.III. Stands characterized by thorny, extremely xeromorphic trees including Blue Palo Verde (*Cercidium floridum,* also known as *Parkinsonia florida*) and Ironwood (*Olneya tesota*).

T.III.A. Stands characterized by Blue Palo Verde (*Cercidium floridum*) as solely dominant in the sparse short tree or tall shrub layer. If Ironwood (*Olneya tesota*) is present, it is significantly less in cover in the tree or shrub layer than *C. floridum.* Characteristic of washes in the lower-elevation (Colorado Desert) portion of the park.
Blue Palo Verde (*Cercidium floridum*) Extremely Xeromorphic Evergreen Shrubland Alliance

Two Associations have been defined from JOTR.

T.III.A.1. Blue Palo Verde forms an open to emergent short tree or tall shrub layer with the constant presence of Desert Lavender (*Hyptis emoryi*) as scattered shorter shrubs.
Blue Palo Verde/Desert Lavender (*Cercidium floridum /Hyptis emoryi*) Association

T.III.A.2. Stands dominated by *Cercidium floridum* in the tree layer. *Hymenoclea salsola* and the Desert Willow (*Chilopsis linearis)* are the most abundant in the shrub layer.
Blue Palo Verde/Desert Willow (*Cercidium floridum/Chilopsis linearis)* Association

T.III.B. Stands characterized by the short tree Desert Ironwood (*Olneya tesota*) strongly dominating an emergent tree layer, often mixed with other tall shrubs. If *Cercidium floridum* is present, it is in substantially lower cover in both tree and shrub layers. Associated with washes and bajadas, with occasional sheet flow in the Colorado Desert portion of the Park.
Desert Ironwood (*Olneya tesota*) Extremely Xeromorphic Evergreen Woodland Alliance (provisional new Alliance)

A single Association has been defined from the park, characterized by the presence of Desert Lavender (*Hyptis emoryi*) in the understory.
Desert Ironwood/Desert Lavender (*Olneya tesota/Hyptis emoryi*) Xeromorphic Woodland Association

T.III.C. Stands characterized by a mixture of Desert Ironwood and Blue Palo Verde, both in relatively low cover as emergent tall shrubs or short trees over desert scrub. Local stands appear to be in fan or bajada settings, without strong wash geomorphology, and relatively low cover of both tall species. Only two plots are assigned to this Alliance currently; no Associations are defined.

Blue Palo Verde-Desert Ironwood *(Cercidium floridum* = *Parkinsonia florida - Olneya tesota)*
Woodland Alliance

Division S: Shrub Vegetation

Vegetation characterized by shrubs of various heights. Trees if present, are usually insignificant (<1 percent cover) and not evenly scattered throughout the stand. This division is categorized into three sections: (1) shrublands of wet to moist localities including springs, seasonally flooded stream channels, and so forth; (2) moderately tall shrublands (shrub canopy ranging from >0.5 m to 4 m) of drier localities from intermittently flooded desert washes to dry uplands; and (3) dwarf shrublands where the average height of shrubs is 0.5 m or less.

Section S.I

S.I. Stands characterized by shrubs of localities remaining wet to moist through the growing season.

S.I.A. Stands characterized by winter-deciduous shrubs of the genus *Salix* (Willows)

> **S.I.A.1.** Narrow-Leaf Willow the dominant shrub. Local stands around freshwater springs scattered throughout the park. No Associations have been defined locally, and no samples taken, but small stands are known from the park.
> **Narrow-Leaf Willow (*Salix exigua*) Deciduous Shrubland Alliance**

S.I.B. Stands characterized by the winter deciduous broom-like shrub, False Willow (*Baccharis sergiloides).* Occasional in upper-elevation canyons and below flowing springs. No Associations defined locally, one sample taken.
False Willow (*Baccharis sergiloides*) Intermittently Flooded Shrubland Alliance

Section S.II

S.II. Stands characterized by a canopy or emergent layer of moderately tall to dwarf shrubs, ranging in a variety of settings from the higher mountains to the lowest portions of the park. This key is based on species composition and contains the largest number of choices in the entire key. A stand is most easily identified if you proceed through all of the choices until you reach a description that fits the characteristics of dominance specified. It is categorized into two subsections, one with Creosote Bush as a common and characteristic component and the other without Creosote Bush as a common and characteristic component.

Subsection S.II.A. Vegetation with Creosote Bush (*Larrea tridentata*) as a characteristic tall shrub (generally >= 1 percent and evenly distributed across the stand). No shrub with cover greater than *Larrea tridentata* with the following exceptions: *Ambrosia dumosa, Encelia farinosa, Krameria* spp. *Bebbia juncea, Ericameria teretifolia* or *Acamptopappus sphaerocephalus. Ephedra nevadensis* may have higher cover, but no more than three times. Go to S.II.A.1.

S.II.A.1. *Ambrosia dumosa* present (>=1 percent cover), may have higher cover than *Larrea tridentata.* If *Encelia farinosa* is present, go to IIA.3. Widespread on all but the hottest and most rocky, sandy, or alkaline areas of the middle and lower elevations.
Creosote Bush - Burro Bush *(Larrea tridentata-Ambrosia dumosa)* Shrubland Alliance

The *Larrea tridentata - Ambrosia dumosa* Shrubland Alliance is one of the most diverse Alliances in the Mojave and Northern Sonoran deserts. It is represented in JOTR by seven Associations, all defined first in this project. In addition to these identified below, there are several other variations that have not been substantiated. These will only be keyable to the Alliance level in the following key:

> **S.II.A.1.a.** Simple, widespread Association with the main two shrubs Creosote Bush and Burro Bush (*Larrea tridentata* and *Ambrosia dumosa)*. No other shrubs common or characteristic.
> **Creosote Bush - Burro Bush (*Larrea tridentata - Ambrosia dumosa)* Shrubland Association**

> **S.II.A.1.b.** Creosote Bush and Burro Bush common with White Rhatany (*Krameria grayi*), a common and characteristic associate.
> **Creosote Bush - Burro Bush - White Rhatany (*Larrea tridentata - Ambrosia dumosa - Krameria grayi)* Shrubland Association**

> **S.II.A.1.c.** Creosote Bush and Burro Bush joined by Schott's Indigo Bush (*Psorothamnus schottii*), often in washes and on bajadas subject to sheet flow in the lower parts of the park including Pinto Basin.
> **Creosote Bush - Burro Bush - Indigo Bush (*Larrea tridentata -Ambrosia dumosa - Psorothamnus schottii)* Shrubland Association**

> **S.II.A.1.d.** Creosote Bush and Burro Bush accompanied by the perennial grass Big Galleta (*Pleuraphis rigida*). Generally present on sandy fans and lower bajadas and occasionally at the edges of sand sheets and dunes.
> **Creosote Bush - Burro Bush - Big Galleta (*Larrea tridentata - Ambrosia dumosa - Pleuraphis rigida)* Shrubland Association**

> **S.II.A.1.e.** Creosote Bush and Burro Bush accompanied by the usually leafless and green-stemmed Desert Senna (*Senna armata*), usually associated with small, sandy washes on mid and lower alluvial fans at middle elevations in the park.
> **Creosote Bush - Burro Bush – Spiny Senna (*Larrea tridentata - Ambrosia dumosa - Senna armata)* Shrubland Association**

> **S.II.A.1.f.** Creosote Bush and Burro Bush accompanied by Mojave Yucca (*Yucca schidigera*) at a cover of less than the total cover of either Creosote Bush or Burro Bush. Common at mid elevations on upper fans and hills in the Mojave Desert portion of the park. If *Y. schidigera* is greater than 2 percent cover with a

comparable cover of Creosote Bush or Burro Bush, the stand falls into the Mojave Yucca Alliance.

Creosote Bush - Burro Bush - Mojave Yucca (*Larrea tridentata - Ambrosia dumosa - Yucca schidigera*) Shrubland Association

S.II.A.1.g. Creosote Bush and Burro Bush accompanied by the short, rounded subshrub Brittlebush (*Encelia farinosa*) at less cover than either *Larrea* or *Ambrosia*. This type usually occurs on lower-elevation slopes in the park. If at mid elevations, it is usually on southerly facing exposures.

Creosote Bush - Burro Bush - Brittlebush (*Larrea tridentata - Ambrosia dumosa - Encelia farinosa*) Shrubland Association

S.II.A.2 *Encelia farinosa* present (>=1 percent cover), may have higher cover than *Larrea tridentata*. *Ambrosia dumosa* may be present but at generally low cover (usually less than *Encelia*). Widespread on hot (southerly exposure) mountain slopes and upper bajadas.

Creosote Bush - Brittlebush (*Larrea tridentata-Encelia farinosa*) Shrubland Alliance

The *Larrea tridentata - Encelia farinosa* Shrubland Alliance is represented by three Associations in JOTR.

S.IIA.2.a. Creosote Bush, Burro Bush, and Brittlebush are all >1 percent cover, and Brittlebush exceeds or equals Burro Bush in cover. Common on lower elevations on neutral, rocky slopes or on steep, south facing slopes at mid elevations throughout the park.

Creosote Bush – Brittlebush - Burro Bush (*Larrea tridentata - Encelia farinosa - Ambrosia dumosa*) Association

S.IIA.2.b. Creosote Bush and Brittlebush are both codominant in the shrub layer with Burro Bush absent or insignificant and no other shrubs in higher cover. This is the simple and common Association of the Alliance on southerly facing slopes at mid elevations throughout the park.

Creosote Bush - Brittlebush (*Larrea tridentata - Encelia farinosa*) Shrubland Association

S.IIA.2.c. Creosote Bush and Brittlebush are both codominant, with the tall, wand-like Ocotillo (*Fouquieria splendens*) as an emergent evenly spaced, though low in cover. Locally distributed on lower fans in Pinto Basin and perhaps elsewhere in the Colorado Desert portion of the park.

Creosote Bush – Brittlebush - Ocotillo (*Larrea tridentata - Encelia farinosa - Fouquieria splendens*) Shrubland Association.

S.II.A.3. Associated shrubs other than *Ambrosia dumosa* or *Encelia farinosa* may be present or absent. Except for shrubs listed above in Subsection IIA, cover of associated shrub species (on an individual basis) is less than *Larrea tridentata*.

Creosote Bush (*Larrea tridentata*) Shrubland Alliance.

There are three Associations identified in the park, along with several single sample variants that, at this point, can only be keyed to the Alliance level.

S.II.A.3.a. Creosote Bush is the sole dominant shrub, with little else in the shrub layer. A monoculture associated with lower bases of fans and bajadas that may be sandy or have had past disturbance (at least, in other parts of the Mojave Desert). **Creosote Bush *(Larrea tridentata)* (Undifferentiated) Shrubland Association**

S.II.A.3.b. Creosote Bush forms a simple shrub layer, with the tufted perennial Big Galleta grass *(Pleuraphis rigida)* evenly distributed in the understory. Generally in sandy areas at lower elevations at the bases of bajadas and adjacent to sand fields.
Creosote Bush - Big Galleta *(Larrea tridentata/Pleuraphis rigida)* Shrubland Association

S.II.A.3.c. Creosote Bush is the sole dominant medium tall shrub, with an even distribution of Cheesebush and few other shrubs. Generally associated with minor washes and disturbed areas in middle to lower elevations of the park.
Creosote Bush - Cheesebush *(Larrea tridentata - Hymenoclea salsola)* Shrubland Association

Subsection S.II.B. Creosote Bush (*Larrea tridentata*), if present, generally not one of the shrub species producing the greatest cover (however, it may be present and even conspicuous). Other shrubs (other than listed in couplet IIA) are typically dominant.

S.II.B.1. Stands characterized (1 percent or higher cover) by the large shrub or small tree Desert Willow *(Chilopsis linearis)*. No other tree-sized or tall shrub species equals or exceeds *Chilopsis linearis* cover. Known from washes at mid to low elevations throughout the park.
Desert Willow *(Chilopsis linearis)* Intermittently Flooded Shrubland Alliance

A single, broadly defined Association is known from the park. *Chilopsis linearis* is the dominant tall shrub or small tree and the less abundant, though constant *Hymenoclea salsola* is in the shrub layer. *Prunus fasciculata* and *Acacia greggii* are nearly as common as *Chilopsis* within a few stands.
Desert Willow (*Chilopsis linearis*) Association

S.II.B.2. Vegetation dominated by tall, shrubby, invasive *Tamarix* spp. (either *T. ramosissima, T. chinensis*, or other similar species but not including the less invasive, taller *T. aphylla*). *Tamarix* spp. should strongly dominate (>60 percent relative cover) over native tall shrubs and/or low trees to be considered as Alliance. Not widespread within the park; in moist environments near springs and streams with semipermanent moisture.
Tamarisk *(Tamarix spp.)* Seminatural Flooded Shrubland Alliance

S.II.B.3. Cheesebush (*Hymenoclea salsola*) >1 percent cover and greater cover than other shrubs. Found commonly in wash environments or disturbed environments. Currently, no Associations are defined in the park. Stands are variable in composition. Stands vary from monospecific to stands with the following species present: *Petalonyx thurberi, Eriogonum plumatella, Salazaria mexicana, Larrea tridentata, Senna armata, Psorothamnus armata*, and *Tetracoccus hallii*.
Cheesebush *(Hymenoclea salsola)* Shrubland Alliance

S.II.B.4. California (or flat-top) Buckwheat (*Eriogonum fasciculatum*) >=2 percent with no other shrub species exceeding it in cover. Usually in disturbed, shallow soils on slopes and pediments near interface with mid- and upper-elevation zones. No Associations defined locally.
California Buckwheat *(Eriogonum fasciculatum)* Shrubland Alliance

S.II.B.5. Bladder-Sage (or Paper-Bag Bush) (*Salazaria mexicana*) >=2 percent cover, with no other shrub species exceeding it in cover. Usually of washes, but may occur on burns or in other disturbed uplands. This Alliance is not defined at the Association level locally.
Bladder-Sage *(Salazaria mexicana)* Shrubland Alliance

S.II.B.6. Mojave Yucca (*Yucca schidigera*) >=2 percent cover. May have other shrub specie, including *Eriogonum fasciculatum, Ephedra nevadensis, Larrea tridentata, Ambrosia dumosa, Tetracoccus hallii*, and *Senna armata*, relatively common. Widespread in the middle elevations of the park, usually on upper fans and hillslopes.
Mojave Yucca *(Yucca schidigera)* Shrubland Alliance

Four Associations have been defined locally.

S.II.B.6.a. Mojave Yucca, often codominant with Blackbush *(Coleogyne ramosissima)*. On pediments and hillslopes near the upper-elevation range of the Alliance.
Mojave Yucca - Blackbush *(Yucca schidigera - Coleogyne ramosissima)* Shrubland Association

S.II.B.6.b. Mojave Yucca associates with Creosote Bush and with Jojoba *(Simmondsia chinensis)*. Occasional on rocky slopes and bajadas near the lower-elevation extent of the alliance.
Mojave Yucca - Creosote Bush - Jojoba *[Yucca schidigera - Larrea tridentata (-Simmondsia chinensis)]* Shrubland Association

S.II.B.6.c. Mojave Yucca associates with Creosote Bush and Burro Bush *(Ambrosia dumosa)*. Common on bajadas and gentle hillslopes at the lower-elevation extent of the alliance near the transition with the Creosote Bush-Burro Bush alliance. In these stands, Mojave yucca is 2 percent or greater cover but may codominate with the other two shrubs.

Mojave Yucca - Creosote Bush - Burro Bush *(Yucca schidigera - Larrea tridentata - Ambrosia dumosa)* Shrubland Association

S.II.B.6.d. Mojave Yucca occurs with several other shrubs and with the perennial Big Galleta grass (*Pleuraphis rigida*). Usually on upper bajadas with a relatively sandy substrate.
Mojave Yucca/Big Galleta (*Yucca schidigera/Pleuraphis rigida)* Shrubland Association

S.II.B.7. *Coleogyne ramosissima* >=2 percent cover. *Ephedra nevadensis* and/or *Krameria grayi* can have up to twice the cover of *Coleogyne ramosissima*. Typically dominates stands, but may be exceeded by species of disturbance (*Hymenoclea salsola, Salazaria mexicana, Ericameria* spp., or *Eriogonum fasciculatum*). A widespread type of shallow, rocky soils on upper bajadas, pediments, and hillslopes. This Alliance is not defined at the Association level locally.
Blackbush *(Coleogyne ramosissima)* Shrubland Alliance

S.II.B.8. Burro Bush (*Ambrosia dumosa*) >1 percent cover, and no other species with equal or higher cover. Occasional on lower, sandy flats or on hillslopes, usually at lower elevations. May occur on edges of washes.
Burro Bush *(Ambrosia dumosa)* Dwarf Shrubland Alliance

A single Association has been defined locally with the perennial Big Galleta grass (*Pleuraphis rigida*) as a conspicuous associate.
Burro Bush - Big Galleta *(Ambrosia dumosa - Pleuraphis rigida)* Dwarf Shrubland Association

S.II.B.9. Brittlebush (*Encelia farinosa*) is dominant (at least >1%), and no other species have equal or higher cover, except possibly *Lycium andersonii*. Occasional on hot, rocky slopes at lower elevations in the park. In the few stands sampled, *Ambrosia dumosa, Lycium andersonii,* and *Fagonia laevis* have been noted as associated species. No Associations have been defined locally.
Brittlebush *(Encelia farinosa)* Shrubland Alliance

S.II.B.10. Anderson's Desert-Thorn or Wolfberry (*Lycium andersonii*) is the dominant species. Usually occurs on rocky slopes at low to mid elevations in scattered locations throughout the park.
Anderson's Boxthorn (*Lycium andersonii*) Shrubland Alliance

This Alliance is represented in the Park by one Association, defined first in this project, the **Anderson's Desert-Thorn – Jojoba - Big Galleta *(Lycium andersonii–Simmondsia chinensis–Pleuraphis rigida)* Shrubland Association**

S.II.B.11. A saltbush species (*Atriplex* spp.) provides >= half of all shrub cover.

S.II.B.11.a. Four-Wing Saltbush (*Atriplex canescens*) with highest shrub cover. Typically of low-lying playa edges, dune aprons, or edges of alkaline wetlands from low- to mid-elevation zones. This Alliance is not defined at the Association level locally.

Four-Wing Saltbush *(Atriplex canescens)* Shrubland Alliance

S.II.B.11.b. Desert Holly *(Atriplex hymenelytra)* >1 percent cover, and no other species with equal or higher cover. May occur on hot, rocky slopes; dry bajadas; or alkaline badlands and playa edges.

Desert Holly *(Atriplex hymenelytra)* Shrubland Alliance

> This Alliance is represented in the park by one Association, defined first in this project.
>
> **Desert Holly - Creosote Bush - Burro Bush *(Atriplex hymenelytra - Larrea tridentata - Ambrosia dumosa)* Shrubland Association**

S.II.B.12. Catclaw *(Acacia greggii)* >=2 percent cover. No other single, tall shrub species with greater cover, but *Prunus fasciculata* or *Hyptis emoryi* may be equal or slightly greater cover than *Acacia.* Smaller shrubs, such as *Ericameria paniculata* or *Hymenoclea salsola,* can have higher cover but no more than twice the cover of *Acacia greggii.* Occurs in washes and arroyos, as well as upland valleys and bouldery slopes. In addition to the following described Associations, this Alliance may also include the following shrub species in some stands that have as yet been undefined at the Association level: *Peucephyllum schottii, Tetracoccus hallii, Ephedra californica, Chilopsis linearis, Ephedra nevadensis, Lycium cooperi, Viguiera parishii, Yucca schidigera, Nolina bigelovii,* and *Eriogonum fasciculatum.*

Catclaw *(Acacia greggii)* Shrubland Alliance

> This Alliance is represented in the park by three Associations, all defined first in this project.

S.II.B.12.a. Catclaw and the shrubby Desert Almond *(Prunus fasciculata)* co-occur, often both codominant in small arroyos and washes on upper fans and in mountains at mid to upper elevations of the park.

Catclaw - Desert Almond *(Acacia greggii - Prunus fasciculata)* Shrubland Association

S.II.B.12.b. Catclaw is the major tall shrub, but Sweetbush *(Bebbia juncea)* is a common short shrub. Generally of rocky washes at lower elevations.

Catclaw - Sweetbush *(Acacia greggii - Bebbia juncea)* Shrubland Association

S.II.B.12.c. Catclaw and Desert lavender *(Hyptis emoryi)* are both common and characteristic. Of lower-elevation, rocky washes and occasionally rocky slopes.

Catclaw - Desert-Lavender *(Acacia greggii - Hyptis emoryi)* Shrubland Association

S.II.B.13. Vegetation either dominated or codominated by California Ephedra *(Ephedra californica),* typically in broad, active washes of mid to upper bajadas and fans. Ranging somewhat locally throughout the southwestern, central, and eastern portions of the area. Other species common in this Alliance include *Hymenoclea salsola, Viguiera parishii,* and *Pleuraphis rigida.*

California Ephedra *(Ephedra californica)* Intermittently Flooded Shrubland Alliance

This Alliance is represented in JOTR by one Association.
California Ephedra *(Ephedra californica)* Shrubland Association

S.II.B.14. Desert Almond (*Prunus fasciculata*) >=2 percent cover. Must be 25 percent or more of total vegetative cover of stand. *Gutierrezia sarothrae* may have higher cover. If *Prunus fasciculata* co-occurs with other tall shrubs, such as *Acacia greggii,* it must have twice the cover of other species to make the Alliance definition. Typically of washes and arroyos at the mid and upper elevations of the park, but may occur on wash terraces and in valleys. The following species are common associates: *Salazaria mexicana, Ericameria teretifolia, Yucca schidigera, Rhus trilobata,* and *Purshia tridentata.*

Desert Almond (*Prunus fasciculata*) Shrubland Alliance

A single, broadly defined Association has been identified from the park.
Desert Almond *(Prunus fasciculata)* Intermittently Flooded Shrubland Association

S.II.B.15. Smoketree (*Psorothamnus spinosus*) >=2 percent cover. No other species with greater or equal cover. Of low-elevation, active washes, mostly in southern and central portion of mapping area. Some of the upper-elevation examples of these stands may have California Buckwheat (*Eriogonum fasciculatum*). The Desert Willow (*Chilopsis linearis*) may occasionally occur in some stands.

Smoketree *(Psorothamnus spinosus)* Intermittently Flooded Shrubland Alliance

This Alliance is represented in JOTR by two Associations.

S.II.B.15.a. Smoketree occurs in stands with Desert Lavender (*Hyptis emoryi*) and Catclaw (*Acacia greggii*). Usually in lower-elevation, rocky washes and arroyos, but may also occur on bouldery slopes.
Smoketree - Desert-Lavender - Catclaw Association *(Psorothamnus spinosus - Hyptis emoryi - Acacia greggii)* Association

S.II.B.15.b. Smoketree occurs in association with Desert Tea *(Ephedra californica).* Usually in sandy washes at mid elevations of the park.
Smoketree/Desert Tea Association *(Psorothamnus spinosus - Ephedra californica)* Association

S.II.B.16. Desert False Willow (*Baccharis sergiloides*), dominant. Typically of intermittent springs and washes in mid and upper elevations, usually in granitic washes and adjacent to springs. This Alliance is not defined at the Association level locally.
Desert False Willow *(Baccharis sergiloides)* Intermittently Flooded Shrubland Alliance

S.II.B.17. Nevada Ephedra (*Ephedra nevadensis*) >=2 percent cover. No other species with greater cover, with the exceptions of *Acamptopappus sphaerocephalus* or *Chrysothamnus viscidiflorus*. This Alliance is not defined at the Association level locally.
Nevada Ephedra (*Ephedra nevadensis)* Shrubland Alliance

S.II.B.18. Rubber Rabbitbrush (*Ericameria nauseosa*) >=2 percent. *Ericameria nauseosa* must have 25 percent or greater relative cover in the shrub layer. Occasional in upper-elevation zones, usually in areas with fire or flood history. This Alliance is not defined at the Association level locally.
Rubber Rabbitbrush *(Ericameria nauseosa)* Shrubland Alliance

S.II.B.19. Paniculate or Black-Stem Rabbitbrush (*Ericameria paniculata*) >=2 percent. *Ericameria paniculata* must be >=25 percent of all cover. Occasional throughout broad elevation range in much of the mapping area in relatively large, recently active washes. This Alliance is not defined at the Association level locally.
Paniculate Rabbitbrush *(Ericameria paniculata)* Intermittently Flooded Shrubland Alliance

S.II.B.20. Round-Leaf Rabbitbrush (*Ericameria teretifolia*) >=2 percent cover. No other species with greater or equal cover. Usually of disturbed uplands, in the upper elevations of the park often adjacent to *Juniperus californica* stands. This Alliance is not defined at the Association level locally.
Round-Leaf Rabbitbrush *(Ericameria teretifolia)* Shrubland Alliance

S.II.B.21. Spiny Hop-Sage (*Grayia spinosa*) >=2 percent cover; no other species with greater cover, except *Ericameria cooperi* or *Lycium andersonii*. *Lycium andersonii* may dominate in some circumstances. *This Alliance has not been formally sampled in the park, but anecdotal evidence suggests that it does locally occur on upper fans and pediments in the middle to higher elevations of the park.*
Spiny Hop-Sage *(Grayia spinosa)* Shrubland Alliance

S.II.B.22. Vegetation characterized by the tall, aromatic shrub Desert Lavender (*Hyptis emoryi)*. Generally, other shrub species are not in high cover, but stands may include *Acacia greggii* and *Sarcostemma cynanchoides*. In rocky washes of upper bajadas and low-elevation canyons throughout the park.
Desert Lavender *(Hyptis emoryi)* Intermittently Flooded Shrubland Alliance

>   This Alliance is represented in the park by one broadly defined Association.
>   **Desert-Lavender *(Hyptis emoryi)* Shrubland Association**

S.II.B.23. Stands dominated by Teddy-Bear Cholla (*(Opuntia bigelovii)*. Local in Pinto Basin on rocky fans.
Teddy-Bear Cholla (*Opuntia bigelovii*) Shrubland Alliance

>   The Alliance is represented locally by a single Association.
>   **Teddy-Bear Cholla *(Opuntia bigelovii)* Shrubland Association**

S.II.B.24. Vegetation characterized by the low diffuse Desert Sunflower or Parish Viguiera (*Viguiera parishii*) with >=2 percent cover. No other species with greater or equal cover. Stands typically occur on rocky hillslopes just above the *Larrea tridentata-Ambrosia dumosa* zone or, rarely, in washes. Other common species in the stands include *Ephedra nevadensis, Hyptis emoryi,* and *Encelia farinosa*.
Parish Viguiera (*Viguiera parishii*) Shrubland Alliance

> This Alliance is represented in the park by one Association, defined first in this project.
> **Parish Viguiera/California Buckwheat *(Viguiera parishii/Eriogonum fasciculatum)* Shrubland Association.** Where California Buckwheat is the most common associate and may codominate.

S.II.B.25. The Yucca-like tall shrub Parry Beargrass (*Nolina parryi*) >3 percent cover. Uncommon, scattered in high portions of the Little San Bernardino Mountains on rocky slopes near other montane Alliances such as Single-Leaf Pinyon (*Pinus monophylla*) and Muller Oak (*Quercus cornelius-mulleri*). No Associations have been defined locally.
Parry Beargrass *Nolina parryi* Shrubland Alliance

S.II.B.26. *Purshia tridentata* >=2 percent cover. If *Artemisia tridentata* or *Ephedra viridis* are present, they have less than 1 percent cover. A local type in high mountains (stands observed occur adjacent to *Juniperus californica* stands on upper fans and near arroyos of the western portion of mapping area. No Associations have been defined locally.
Antelope Bush *(Purshia tridentata)* Shrubland Alliance

S.II.B.27. Vegetation characterized by Muller or Desert Scrub Oak (*Quercus cornelius-mulleri*). The oak is > or + 2 percent cover and is not exceeded by any tree cover such as California Juniper or Single-Leaf Pinyon Pine.
Muller Oak (*Quercus Cornelius-mulleri*) Shrubland Alliance

> Two Associations have been defined locally.

> **S.II.B.27.a.** Muller Oak is the dominant overstory shrub over a scattered, shorter shrub layer characterized by Linear-Leafed Goldenbush (*Ericameria linearifolia*) and California Buckwheat (*Eriogonum fasciculatum*). Common on slopes of higher mountains.
> **Muller Oak/California Buckwheat - Linear-Leafed Goldenbush (*Quercus cornelius-mulleri/Eriogonum fasciculatum-Ericameria linearifolia*) Shrubland Association**

> **S.II.B.27.b.** Muller Oak occurs with the shorter shrub Blackbush (*Coleogyne ramosissima*) on upper fans and relatively linear hillslopes of the upper elevations.
> **Muller's Oak/Blackbush (*Quercus cornelius-mulleri/Coleogyne ramosissima*) Shrubland Association**

S.II.B.28. Bigberry Manzanita (*Arctostaphylos glauca*), dominant, at least 2 percent cover with no other shrub species equaling or exceeding it in cover. Occasional stands on high and relatively warm slopes of the Little San Bernardino Mountains. No Associations defined locally.
Bigberry Manzanita (*Arctostaphylos glauca*) Shrubland Alliance

S.II.B.29. Stands dominated by the Euphorbiaceous shrub *Tetracoccus hallii*. Stands are generally centered in the southern-central portion of the park from low-elevation wash margins near the Eagle Mine to rocky uplands in the vicinity of Cottonwood Springs. Insufficient information exists to define an Alliance, so these stands are considered unique at this point.
Hall's Tetracoccus *(Tetracoccus hallii)* Unique Stands

S.II.B.30. Stands dominated by the large shrub known as Lotebush *(Ziziphus obtusifolia)*. Stands occur adjacent to small washes in the southern portion of the park near Cottonwood Springs and, so far, are not known elsewhere.
Lotebush (*Ziziphus obtusifolia*) Unique Stands (one plot)

S.IIB.31. Stands are distinguished by the dominance of the Chuparosa (*Justicia californica*). Occasional stands associated with low-elevation washes at the southern portion of the park near other stands of Colorado Desert wash vegetation (*Olneya tesota* and *Cercidium floridum* Alliance stands or *Hyptis emoryi* stands). So far, not described elsewhere and currently treated as unique stands.
Chuparosa *(Justicia californica)* Unique Stands

Division H: Herbaceous Vegetation

Two sections are included: (1) perennial grasslands and (2) annual grasslands.

Section H.I

H.I. Stands dominated by perennial grasses.
Perennial Grasslands

H.IA. Big Galleta Grass (*Pleuraphis rigida*) >=2 percent. This species occurs in low, sandy areas and occasionally uplands at mid elevations, often with emergent shrubs such as *Yucca schidigera* and *Ephedra nevadensis*. As an Alliance in the park, it is generally uncommon in upland areas, such as upper bajadas, sandy washes, and intermontane valleys, and somewhat more common in low, sandy areas. In addition to the Association described below, several stands include several shrubs such as *Hymenoclea salsola*, *Lycium cooperi,* and *Ephedra nevadensis* in total lower cover than the grass cover. Other unclassified stands suggest a relatively pure Association with little other perennial cover but Big Galleta.
Big Galleta *(Pleuraphis rigida)* Herbaceous Alliance

This Alliance is represented in the park by one Association, first described for this project. It is characteristic of low flats adjacent to sandy playas, such as Pleasant Valley, and characterized by the presence of scattered shrubs of Four-wing Saltbush.
Big Galleta -Four-wing *(Pleuraphis rigida - Atriplex canescens)* Grassland Association

H.IB. Vegetation characterized by the dominance of the bunch grass Desert Needlegrass *(Achnatherum speciosum).* Rare in mapping area, usually in small enclaves surrounded by more extensive upland vegetation of mid- to upper-elevation Alliances such as *Coleogyne ramosissima* Shrubland. No Associations defined.
Desert Needlegrass *(Achnatherum speciosum)* Herbaceous Alliance

Section H.II

H.II. Stands dominated by annual grasses, locally in all cases, these species are nonnatives. Stands fluctuate, depending on annual variation in timing and amount of precipitation. No perennial species (either shrubs or herbs) totaling greater than 10 percent absolute cover.
Annual Grasslands

H.IIA. Vegetation dominated by Cheatgrass (*Bromus tectorum*). Occasional in postburn situations, mostly at mid and upper elevations and associated with former stands of *Yucca brevifolia, Pinus monophylla, Coleogyne ramosissima,* and *Juniperus californica* Alliances.
Cheatgrass (*Bromus tectorum*) Annual Herbaceous Alliance

H.IIB. Vegetation dominated by Red Brome (*Bromus madritensis* ssp. *rubens*). Generally present in disturbed areas in middle elevations of the park.
Red Brome (*Bromus madritensis* ssp. *rubens*) Annual Herbaceous Alliance

NPS 909/107410, April 2011